LOL

LOVE OTHERS LOUDLY

"LET ALL THAT YOU DO,
BE DONE IN LOVE"

1 Corinthians 16:14

MARK McCUEN

LOL – Love Others Loudly

© 2020 Mark McCuen, LOL-Ministries, LLC.

Requests for information should addressed to:
information@lol-ministries.com

Library of Congress Cataloging-in-Publication Data
McCuen, Mark, 1955 –
LOL – Love Others Loudly / Mark McCuen

ISBN: 978-0-9788659-5-5

Design: Amadeo Reverisco Publishing
Edited by Annie K. Preston

Morgan Wynn Publishing
Morgan Wynn Publishing Phoenix, AZ 85071

Printed in the United States of America

About the Author ...

If you have ever had the privilege, and joy!, of watching some-one grow and mature you will understand how I feel about my relationship with author Mark McCuen. We met several years ago at **One Church Scottsdale**, where I teach **Sunday University**, an adult Bible Study class. Though a Christian for 50 years plus, Mark was *Un-Churched, Un-Hymned,* and *Un-Bibled.* He knew that he Loved Jesus, but knew little about how that Love should be manifested.

Mark immersed himself in the Word of God and just couldn't get enough of it. He found he had been part of the situation found in **Hebrews 5:12** CEV – *"By now you should have been teachers, but once again you need to be taught the simplest things about what God has said. You need milk instead of solid food."*

Mark shared with me that as he delved into the scriptures it was as though his whole life unfolded before him in a completely new context. For the first time ever, not only did he know all of the "what," he was beginning to understand many of the "whys!"

From these self-discoveries, *Love Others Loudly* emerged. It is a compilation of the life events of a Christian who had no idea what being a Christian was all about. Mark had known, and recognized, the Blessings he had enjoyed as a Christian. He realized that he had even been living out many Christian principles, though he had no idea what those principles were. *Love Others Loudly* is a text that you will not only enjoy reading but will benefit from having done so as well!

Floyd Allen, Editor
MORGAN WYNN PUBLISHING

Mark & Kayleen McCuen

LOVE, THE GREATEST GIFT

"If I speak with the tongues
of men and of angels,
but do not have love,
I have become a noisy gong
or a clanging cymbal.

If I have the gift of prophecy,
and know all mysteries
and all knowledge;
and if I have all faith,
so as to remove mountains,
but do not have love,
I am nothing.

And if I give all my possessions
to feed the poor, and if I surrender
my body to be burned,
but do not have love,
it profits me nothing.

Love is patient, love is kind
and is not jealous; love does not brag
and is not arrogant,
does not act unbecomingly;
it does not seek its own,
is not provoked,
does not take into account a wrong
suffered, does not rejoice
in unrighteousness,
but rejoices with the truth;

ACKNOWLEDGEMENTS:

Five years ago, the notion of writing a book was not even a thought. After recently surviving heart failure, back surgery, and life-threatening brain surgery, my only thoughts were about recovery. In fact, the only thing that could hold my attention in 2015 was watching my beloved Iowa Hawkeyes in their historic undefeated season. My brain surgery in 2014 had left me with limited use of my hands and feet. The thrill of watching the Hawkeyes win twelve straight games was a welcome distraction from the countless visits for needed physical rehabilitation.

As a result of the emergency brain surgery, my hands would no longer do simple tasks like pick up a dime from the table. For me, being able to type a book was equivalent to climbing Mount Everest. Explaining how my typing skills before the surgery were non-existent and describing my "hunt and peck" approach to typing, didn't stop my persistent Physical Therapist who was adamant that typing would help. So, at her behest, the typing began.

Remembering a career of marketing and all the words that had passed through my fingers only added to my frustration. For decades, writing was work not pleasure. Writing all those words that were never read. Words describing the latest greatest technology that the reader needed to buy, right now! Words that were swallowed up in innumerable brochures, PowerPoints, and "blurbs."

Starting by writing some family history and posting them on my "blog" was a chore. Every day seemed to be a battle between my index fingers and the spell checker. The futile task brought back memories of my mom telling me to take typing in high school. Not extremely high on my list of priorities in those days. Only six years after the brain surgery, my résumé now includes the title "author." Go figure.

(Love)

bears all things, believes all things,
hopes all things, endures all things.

Love never fails;
but if there are gifts of prophecy,
they will be done away;
if there are tongues, they will cease;
if there is knowledge,
it will be done away.

For we know in part
and we prophesy in part;
but when the perfect comes,
the partial will be done away.

When I was a child,
I used to speak like a child,
think like a child, reason like a child;
when I became a man,
I did away with childish things.

For now we see in a mirror dimly,
but then face to face;
now I know in part,
but then I will know fully
just as I also have been fully known.

But now faith, hope,
love, abide these three;
but the greatest of these is love."

1 Corinthians 13 NAS

There is so much gratitude in my heart, it is overflowing with names and circumstances to acknowledge. With that, my OCD (obsessive compulsive disorder) took over with a strong desire to categorize and catalog each one. Well, that would require another book. So, in an attempt to tell everyone thanks, the following is a list of categories and first names (you should know who you are) of those that helped, influenced, prodded, pestered and encouraged the creation of this book.

God: Without my God, His spirit and beloved son Christ Jesus in my life, it would have been impossible. With Him, all things are possible. Thank you Abba, Alpha & Omega, El Deah, El Elyon, El Olam, El Shaddai, Jehovah, Elohim, Yahweh, Yahweh-Raah, Yahweh-Shalom, Yahweh-Yireh, Christos, Deliverer, Good Shepherd, Immanuel, King of Kings, Lord of Lords, Host of Hosts, Lamb of God, Messiah, I Am.

Family: My beloved bride, Kayleen. Our wonderful children and their partners, Jason, Melissa, Jennifer, Alex, Jaclyn, Erik & James. Our three grandsons, Lowan, Connor and Sullivan. My Mom and Dad, Gwen, Bob, Jody, Wayne, Michael, Shannon, Lindsay, Jaron, Erin, Kevin, Beth, Josh, Lisa, Jesse, Belinda, Karla, Taleah, Josh, Brandi, Travis, Mike, Michelle, Charley, Robyn, Maranda, Mikie, Mitchell, Mary, Cindy, Joanie, Martha, Gene, Brion, Erin, Colan, Annie, Mike and Malesha.

Pastors, Teachers & Mentors in Christ: Hume, Alec, Rita, Mack, Jo, Doug, Gary, JoAnne, Rowdy, Ashli, Bob, Elouise, Floyd, Clarissa, Steve, Matt, Margie, Ed, Shara, Mark, Britt, Bill, Shelia, Michael, Travis, Ken, Trammel, Eric, Lori, Art, Erick, Billy, Steve, BJ, Jason, Tom, Elizabeth, Carlos, Will, Perry, Maradell, JoAnne, Dan, Israel, Bart, Amy, Lauren, Ryan, Dave, Meredith, Jason, Rick, Kay, Andy, Robert, Rankin & Andrew.

Friends: Too many to list, …

My Editor: Annie (She's the BEST!)
Thank you all from the bottom of my Heart!

LOVEOTHERSLOUDLY

Prologue 9

LOVE GOD FIRST   **12**

Faith   *Let Go of the Rope*   14

Focus   *A Point in Every Direction is Point Less*   24

Gratitude   *Give Thanks in All That You Do*   36

LOVE PEOPLE GRATEFULLY   **58**

Devotion   *Love with Commitment*   60

Encouragement   *Be Nice to People on the Way Up*   72

Awareness   *The Love you Take, Equals the Love You Make*   88

LOVE PEOPLE WITH COMPASSION   **102**

Empathy   *Savior or Servant?*   104

Understanding   *Sympathy or Empathy?*   120

Trust   *A Reason to Believe*   140

LOVE PEOPLE WITH CONVICTION   **154**

Clarity   *Truth or Consequences?*   156

Courage   *There is No Growth Without Friction*   170

Passion   *No Wise Man Can Reason Away Belief*   184

Epilogue 202

Scripture References 210

IS LOVE ALL WE NEED? ...

In Christ we are taught to "Love One Another." How does that work? It seems to be an impossible directive. When Jesus taught to love our neighbors as ourselves, did he really know about that guy that lives next door? How can we truly love ALL our neighbors? Certainly, there must be some people that God would give us a pass on. God must know my neighbor can be a jerk.

For those who don't follow Christ, doesn't society mandate us to be kind, to love each other? Love permeates our culture. It is in our music, those warm fuzzy TV commercials, and at the movies. It seems we are surrounded by a Love edict. Growing up in the sixties, my generation was nicknamed the "Love Generation," where we declared love was free, and it was all we needed. We even dedicated an entire season to it: The "Summer of Love." One of my favorite bands in the sixties, The Beatles, taught us that "All You Need is Love" and that love was the answer to most of the problems of the world. John Lennon's famous quote, "Love is the Answer. What was the Question?" said it all.

If we humans are so fixated on love, why is there so much hate and vitriol in the world? Sadly, even inside of our church communities, love seems to be idle, giving way to divisiveness, competition, and separation from others. Love has been examined, dissected, and philosophized about since the first human walked the planet. We have been taught there are multiple versions of love; variations based on language, psychological perception, and biblical interpretations.

Each explanation breaks love into multiple descriptions. Are we over-analyzing love into obscurity? The smaller the variant, the less significant each piece is.

Don't we work to "divide and conquer" most things that we don't understand or can't control?

Throughout my life, loving my fellow man has been the anchor in my relationships; personally, casually, and in my career. Not one love for this person, and another type of love for someone else. Instead, my goal was to always lead with unconditional love. That is, love without requirements, specifications, or expectations of reciprocation. Not always an easy path.

Love Others Loudly is the story of how love has always worked in my life and is still at the core of all my interactions with others. How leading with unconditional love guided my steps; keeping me focused on the needs of others and not myself. A path that took a high school dropout working 12 hours a day in a dirty warehouse in Des Moines, Iowa, to the senior management staff of a Fortune 500 company and beyond.

"God blesses us, not for ourselves,

... He blesses us so that we may bless others."

~Rowdy Van Horn, Pastor, One Church, Scottsdale

LOVE LOUDLY!

LOVE GOD & LOVE PEOPLE!

LoveOthersLoudly

SECTION

"So love the Lord your God with all your heart, soul, and strength."

Deuteronomy 6:5

Love GOD First!

FAITH

LET GO OF THE ROPE!

CHAPTER 1

"WE MUST HOLD TIGHTLY
TO THE HOPE WE SAY
IS OURS. AFTER ALL,
WE CAN TRUST THE
ONE WHO MADE THE
AGREEMENT WITH US."
HEBREWS 10:23 CEV

Who Controls Your Life?

Aren't we all looking for that KEY? The KEY that
unlocks all the mysteries of life, that opens the
door to an unrestricted existence? One simple
understanding that lifts the burden of obligation.
Ah, to never have to balance a checkbook again!

That perfect relationship with that perfect
person. To find complete acceptance in any social
situation. Never wondering, how I am going to do
that? How do I fit in? or **What do 'they' think?**

FAITH

Getting the KEY is often a monumental step, albeit daunting. Dad giving you the KEYS to the family car, the Realtor giving you the KEY to your first house. Your boss giving you a KEY to your first private office - or getting the KEY to your first business. As the cycle continues, handing your car KEYS to your sixteen-year-old son or daughter. **Daunting indeed!**

In Christ, are we too comfortable, believing we have things completely figured out? Still, we need to balance checkbooks, maintain healthy relationships with friends and loved ones and steer clear of falling victim to peer pressure. Knowing that we are a continual work in progress, most of us who live in Christ strive to be better every day. However, life can be tough. While we work to apply all we learn in scripture, it seems the world continues to punch us in the face.

> "FAITH ISN'T THE ABILITY TO
> BELIEVE LONG AND FAR INTO
> THE MISTY FUTURE. IT'S SIMPLY
> TAKING GOD AT HIS WORD
> AND TAKING THE NEXT STEP."
>
> Joni Erickson Tada

Like most of you, my life has been full of problems, pressures, and conflicts. For decades, through it all, God has been working with me, covering me while lighting my path. Teaching me to come closer to Him and farther away from the stuff of the world. Looking back through the turmoil, God has shown me a simple understanding that has helped tremendously in my life, eliminating a host of hardships.

Do you remember playing "tug o' war" as a kid? Maybe you still play. It's been a while for me, but it was one of my favorite games. A ruckus team sport that was usually played over a muddy pit. Initially, we believed that the game was winnable only through brute strength. As our team got better, we realized it was more of a "head" game.

Turns out that "tug o' war" was all about strategy and how to take the best advantage of the strength available. Our strategies always included "psyching out" our opponents before the match. Mainly, so that they would start the game doubting their abilities. However, my favorite move was what we called the "fake out." That glorious move occurred when all at once, our team would give some slack in the rope to the other team. Instantly thinking they "had" us, the other team would often let up at the first sign of relaxing the rope.

"But seek first His kingdom and His righteousness, and all these things will be added to you. ..."

Matthew 6:33

With a shout, our team would pull back with everything we had, "hooking" them like a fish on the line. We won more matches with that move than any other.

You might be wondering, what does "tug o' war" have to do with a KEY to life's problems? Think of it as a simple analogy of our walk with God. We start out thinking that our "Brute Strength" will get us through life. Then, when we accept Christ as our savior and learn more about God's grace, we come to understand that when things go wrong, we must submit all to Christ. Do we submit? Completely?

FAITH

Do you find complete surrender hard to do?

Whether we are pulling on the rope, asking God for what WE believe WE need, or even in those times when we truly give it all to God, praying, "Your Will, Not Mine," don't we still tend to hold on tightly to the rope; fully ready to yank back when WE believe it's needed? Isn't THE KEY to let go of the rope? To truly give all our troubles and life to God? It is only in our complete surrender and obedience to God that, as He promised, we will find the peace that surpasses all understanding.

> "GOD USES HIS WORD,
> PEOPLE, AND CIRCUMSTANCES
> TO MOLD US."
>
> Pastor Rick Warren

In my experience, it's all about trust. Trusting God to take us by the hand so that when we let go of the rope, we don't fall. The more we trust God, the more we see what He does in our lives. The more we see what He does in our lives, the more we trust Him.

Throughout my life, when letting go of the rope and letting God have it, He has never let me down. When we weren't sure where the next dollar was coming from, where we would live, how we would find food to eat... Giving it all to God, He always had our backs. Without fail. We weren't dripping in money, gold, and diamonds, but He always provided.

Starting my career in a dusty warehouse, it seemed my life was never going to match my dreams. Scared and frustrated, my fear led me to give it all to God, asking for guidance and help. Looking back, it was a single event — dropping out of school — that led me to meet the love of my life, my bride now, for over 45 years. Unquestionably, the biggest earthly blessing of my life. Through some very tough years, God provided and ordered our steps into a wonderful and blessed life together.

Recently, when giving up alcohol and pain pills, once more, God led me to my knees, fearing the loss of everything. Again, giving it all to God and begging for His help, He not only grabbed my hand, taking me out of my addictions, but from that day forward, all desire for alcohol and opioids were gone. Wiped out entirely. That is the God Factor for me. When you give it all completely to Him, fear, doubt, and anxiety go away. Completely.

So many times, even in my walk with Christ, desire to control the outcome led me to plan things on my own. Not giving it to God always seemed to lead me into

> With all your heart you must trust the LORD and not your own judgment.
>
> Proverbs 3:5 CEV

chaos. Sure, my thoughts and prayers were with God, always asking for help; but it was too easy to give in to MY plans and MY understanding, and not His will. Things might have worked, and sometimes even gotten better, but it was never without strife and disorder. Looking back, it was me holding on to the rope that created the chaos while working to control the outcome.

Letting go of the rope continues to be a battle for me. God has taught me that it's ALL about trust and faith. Believing that God will grab my hand, place me on His solid rock, and see me through. He has always been there for me.

18

FAITH

"FAITH IS TAKING THE FIRST
STEP EVEN WHEN YOU DON'T
SEE THE WHOLE STAIRCASE."

Martin Luther King, Jr.

LOVE In**ACTION**
STRENGTH OF FAITH

You might be thinking, Sure "Letting Go of the Rope" is easy for you. But my circumstances are different. If I let go of my finances, how will the bills get paid? If we don't force our kids to do what we believe is right, they'll wander into the things of the world. Or, my favorite, Why, I could never do that, I'm just not strong enough!

Trust me, those words, and many more, have crossed my lips. It is vital to always remember that fear is NOT of God. Giving into fear creates a chasm between us and God. My fear and anxiety led me to so many bad decisions that it would take volumes to detail every single one. Please know that like you, so many times my life seemed unmanageable and wrought in chaos; leading me to Yank Back On the Rope, in hopes that my plans, driven by fear and anxiety, would see me through the problem. Sometimes the plans would work, most times they didn't. In all cases, they would increase anxiety and often created new fears.

> And without faith it is impossible to please Him,
> For he who comes to God must believe that He is and that He is a rewarder of those who seek Him.
>
> Hebrews 11:6

Over time, in prayer, meditation, and study of scripture, it became clear that the answer to ALL of life's problems are found in the complete, unconditional surrender to God, with unceasing obedience.

FAITH

It took me decades of anxiety, pain and suffering to begin to follow God's will. Finding His will in scripture led me to complete surrender and obedience. Toughest lesson of my life.

When facing the unknown and unseen path ahead of us, it is in our human nature to predict and figure out what's going to happen. So often, it is this curiosity and knowledge that leads us to try to control the outcome on our own. Much like the proverbial "back seat driver," we think that all our yelling, sound effects and superior insight will alter the path of the driver, when in truth we are more often creating a distraction and not helping.

> "HAVE FAITH IN GOD;
> GOD HAS FAITH IN YOU."
>
> Edwin Louis Cole

It is our brain and our knowledge that will lead us into fear and doubt. As scripture tells us over and over, we are NOT to lean on our own understanding. Instead, we must lean on God. Completely!

If you are afraid of heights, what is it that drives your fear? Are you truly afraid of the distance, or is it more that you are afraid of hitting the ground after a long fall? Isn't it the knowledge of gravity and your experience with pain that drives your fear? If you knew nothing of gravity and the pain of hitting the ground, would you be afraid?

Working to not always think about what could happen, letting MY understanding control my life always reminds me of the scripture that tells us that we must change and be like little children. Children don't have the knowledge or experience to be afraid. Their trust is strengthened by their lack of knowledge, not by their understanding. Most children do not seek to control their situation. It is only when giving ALL to God, trusting Him, that He will give us the peace that surpasses ALL understanding.

LOVE GOD FIRST BY:

"Putting ALL of Your Faith and Trust in Him!"

Jesus called for a child to come over and stand near him. Then he said: I promise you this. If you don't change and become like a child, you will never get into the kingdom of heaven.

Matthew 18:2-3 CEV

FOCUS

A POINT IN EVERY DIRECTION
IS POINT LESS ...

CHAPTER 2

"WITH ALL YOUR HEART
YOU MUST TRUST THE
LORD AND NOT YOUR
OWN JUDGMENT."
PROVERBS 3:5 CEV

Do Your Desires Consume You?

Why do we lose our direction ... our **Focus?**

It seems that we frequently lose sight of what is important in our lives. Often, we convince ourselves, rationalizing what we are fixated on, is the best thing, even when we know in our heart it will lead us astray.

Why do we do that?

We're human.

24

Focus

Decades ago, God and my career led me to the Publishing Industry, working with a small start-up in Philadelphia that was a cornerstone in the Desktop Publishing Revolution. We were engulfed in one of my first "Industry Disruptions." Every day was a new adventure in how this new technology could, and would, obliterate technologies and entrenched practices. One of my favorite experiences during my career were the two weeks spent at the National Enquirer offices in Florida. My job? Interview everyone involved in the paper's production … from writers and editors to page compositors and color specialists. We even talked with the legal department that protected the paper from lawsuits. The experience was eye opening at so many levels. It set the stage for my unique understanding of the industry.

> "FOCUS ON GIANTS
> YOU STUMBLE.
> FOCUS ON GOD
> YOUR GIANTS TUMBLE."
>
> Max Lucado - Facing Your Giants

Cheeseburgers or Paradise?

In 1988, media mogul, Generoso Paul "Gene" Pope Jr., creator of the National Enquirer that we know today, had succumbed to a heart attack at the age of 61. After his death, his family sold the paper to a publisher in New York City that was one of our best customers. At our customer's request, we were sent to prepare a proposal bringing the manually created paper into the Twentieth Century with automated publishing.

During my interviews with the Enquirer staff, there was story after story of their founder they lovingly referred to as Pope. By all accounts, Pope was a genius. Like most geniuses it has been my pleasure to know, he had some idiosyncrasies. For example, people told me that he had never made the internationally distributed newspaper a corporation, paying personal income tax on the multi-million-dollar company instead. When asked why he didn't just incorporate and save the potential millions of dollars in tax relief, he quipped, *"How many cheeseburgers can you eat?"* There was clearly no greed nor guile in his heart. His focus was not on the money, nor power. He had a vision and a passion that guided his steps while not seeing the lost money as a problem.

We humans are problem solvers. Whether you believe in God or not, the human history of solving problems has given our species a unique track record of accomplishment. Non-believers look at the invention of fire, the wheel, and the industrial revolution as huge milestones in the human quest to become the dominant species on the planet. On the other hand, people who believe in divine

> For as he thinks within himself, so he is. He says to you, "Eat and drink!" But his heart is not with you.
>
> **Proverbs 23:7**

creation, when asked, will typically point to God as the architect of all human innovation, even though believers can often be found patting themselves on the back for human progress, thinking, *"Look what we (or I) accomplished!"* After all, don't we often show our arrogance in how we treat our planet and other species? The cliché, "Holier Than Thou," always comes to mind. Whether it's a kid stepping on an ant hill or grown men betting on a dog or chicken fight. Our superior "haughty" view of the world is sometimes pitifully crystal clear. Still, we reason it away as a solution. Hitler even called the genocide of the holocaust the "Final Solution," while touting, *"The end justifies the means!"*

In elementary school, my favorite subject was Native American culture. At the time, my studies focused on the Oglala tribe, and the rest of the Dakota Sioux Nation of the American Plains. The North Plains Nations spawned Sitting Bull, Crazy Horse, and Red Cloud – the leaders of a huge indigenous culture. These nations, against all odds, took on the invading armies of the east. While they were no match for the onslaught of man and machine that was bearing down on them, those primitive people put up such a valiant fight that their tactics are still talked about and taught in military schools today.

> "LACK OF DIRECTION, ...
> NOT LACK OF TIME, ...
> IS THE PROBLEM.
> WE ALL HAVE
> TWENTY-FOUR-HOUR DAYS."
>
> Zig Ziglar

Who was Savage?

In the same vein as William Wallace of "Braveheart" fame, the Oglala and Dakota Sioux were not fighting to hold onto wealth or belongings. They were fighting for their culture, their very existence. Regrettably, both were swallowed up by technologically advanced invaders. The supposedly enlightened invaders were focused on their civilization's solution; that is, the complete dominance of their culture over all others. Any person or culture that got in their way was assimilated ... much like the haughty spirit of the child stepping on the ant hill. The invading forces didn't understand that while they were acquiring more land and expanding their civilization, they were annihilating an entire culture.

When God introduced me to the Oglala and Dakota Sioux while writing a book report about General George A. Custer and his defeat by the so-called savages, something wonderful happened. God showed me who these great people really were, and they were anything but savages. In relaying my newfound wisdom in class, the giggles began. Students and teachers alike would ridicule my comments, teaching me lessons that altered my life. Lessons that might warrant another story or perhaps even a book of their own.

At the core of my new understanding was a deep respect for the way of life enjoyed on the plains before the invasion from the east. Sure, indigenous plains living was void of luxuries, houses, furniture or ready-made clothing, but every individual in these tightly knit communities supported one another, unconditionally. Some were hunters and some made tents, while others served the tribe by whatever skill they were blessed with.

> Looking at them, Jesus said, "With people it is impossible, but not with God; for all things are possible with God."
> Mark 10:27

Being human, they were intelligent and had a very human violent side. The brutal tactics used in their protection were the foundation of all the "savage" stories propagated by the invaders. Why were they so savage? They were being invaded. For the most part, the stories in my studies talked more about protecting families and a way of life, than the unrestrained destruction and gruesome violence we learned about in school or at the movies. It was their way of life that attracted me to better understand who these "savages" were. Simply said, they were loving, kind people who always served one

28

another, and ALWAYS gave glory to their creator for the gifts provided to them. It seems we Christians could learn a thing or two from them.

Reading story after story of their love and respect for each other, and the unquestioning love and respect for their creator, drew me close to their way of life. Nothing was wasted, all life was sacred. When the hunters would bring home a Buffalo, every bit of the Buffalo was used for something. Meat to eat, tents and clothing made of hide, even cooking utensils and weapons were fashioned from Buffalo bone. In honor and respect of the "gift," everything was used. Like my mom always said, *"Waste Not, Want Not!"* It was this culture that taught me to be a conservationist, full of love and respect for our beautiful planet, God's gift to us all.

> "TELL ME WHAT YOU EAT,
> AND I WILL TELL YOU
> WHAT YOU ARE."
>
> Jean Anthelme Brillat-Savarin

The foundation of the culture was a populace that gave thanks for everything, from the sun rising and setting each day to the ground that they walked on. Initially, some were thankful for these new neighbors from the east. Well, until we taught them otherwise. You may be wondering why these great nations could not find victory over their oppressors. My belief is they were not fighting an oppressor, they were fighting for their sacred lifestyle. It wasn't important to them to hang on to property and belongings. Instead, their lives were dedicated to staying in harmony with their creator. Life and all the gifts of their world were cherished above any and all possessions. This led to compliance with their invaders, and eventually they were defeated and absorbed into western culture.

Not unlike the Israelites in scripture, some held onto their culture and passed it down through generations in folklore and storytelling. The culture is still understood and practiced and is seeing a renaissance. Today we see a proud people reclaiming their position from within the imperious capitalist culture that engulfed them. While most have lost their focus, the way of life is still alive. If Sitting Bull knew the culture endured, it would bring a smile to that stone-etched face.

You might be thinking, *"What does any of this have to do with cheeseburgers?"* Simply said, the eastern invaders were chasing cheeseburgers, and the great Native American cultures were seeking to protect their paradise.

> Seek the LORD and His strength; Seek His face continually.
> 1 Chronicles 16:11

Given a choice, wouldn't most of us choose quality of life over quantity of things? Would we give up our fast cars, smart phones and $5 coffee for a blissful life, spending every day living in harmony with everyone and everything around us, while honoring our creator? Could we find joy? Regrettably, we are what we eat.

Would we choose cheeseburgers or paradise? We love our fast food! Paradise seems like a great idea, but is it fun? Can we get there **Right Now?!** Leaving our stomachs out of it for now, isn't what we focus on every day considered a consumption as well? If we spend all our time thinking about the next fast car, the next generation phone and the need for that expresso, isn't it consuming us? So often we hear, "As a man thinketh, so is he." We believe the often-misquoted scripture is all about changing our thinking, recreating our brain. It's not! The Bible teaches us over and over that we are consumed by what is in our heart, not our brain. It is our desire and what is in our heart that drives us.

You might be wondering, *"If living a blissful life means total annihilation by your enemies, no thanks."* Do you believe that if the Native Americans had only focused on their enemy and the destruction of their culture, they could have stopped it? Much like that "back-seat driver" screaming before a car wreck, the outcome was inevitable. As humans, we often believe we can control an outcome. As Christians we should know, as scripture tells us, with man, it is impossible; but with God, ALL things are possible.

"IS PRAYER YOUR STEERING WHEEL OR YOUR SPARE TIRE?"

Corrie ten Boom

It is in our personal prayers that we let go of our life and begin to trust God. As holocaust survivor, Corrie ten Boom, taught; *"We need to pray continually, in a never ceasing conversation with God."* It is in prayer that we are led to find love in all we do. The Fruit of the Spirit is Love. Scripture shows us that it is not our job to make fruit. That's God's job! In prayer, with our eyes focused on God, following His will, we are blessed with the fruit as a gift. When we stop giving, we stop getting. Spreading the gift of love throughout the world through prayer and obedience will guide our every step.

It seems the hardest thing for humans to do is to let go of the things of this world, and, with unconditional faith, let God handle it. Like those native cultures that focused on their creator, and the blessings they were given. Shouldn't we keep our eyes, thoughts, and desires focused on our God? It is then, we will find the love, joy, and peace promised in His word.

Therefore we also, since we are
surrounded by so great a cloud
of witnesses, let us lay aside
every weight, and the sin
which so easily ensnares us,
and let us run with endurance
the race that is set before us,
fixing our eyes on Jesus,
the author and perfecter of faith,
who for the joy set before Him
endured the cross,
despising the shame, and
has sat down at the right hand
of the throne of God.

Hebrews 12:1-2

32

FOCUS

"EVEN WHEN IT FEELS AS IF WE
ARE BEING CRUSHED BY EARTHLY
TROUBLES, WE CAN REMAIN
JOYFUL. IF WE KEEP OUR FOCUS
ON GOD, OUR SPIRIT
CANNOT BE TRAMPLED."

Mary C. Neal - To Heaven and Back

33

LOVE IN ACTION

FOCUS ON GOD

If you're like me, your days are so full it seems that there is not enough time in the day. In today's fast paced world, we are confronted with one emergency after another. Spending our lives fighting fires everywhere we turn. There you are in the middle of a house burning down fighting the current fire. Someone runs in screaming, "There's a fire next door!" What do you do? If you leave the current fire, the house will go up in smoke. If you don't go next door, that house will be destroyed. Such is the life of a Fire Fighter. You are constrained to fight one fire at a time.

As an experienced firefighter, you might believe that you have it all under control. Reasoning it through, you go to the window and begin to spray the house next door, thinking, "Thank God for

> For the mind set on the flesh is death, but the mind set on the Spirit is life and peace,
>
> **Romans 8:6**

multitasking." Once the fire goes down next door, you turn your hose back to the house you're in. Problem is there is only one stream of water. Eventually, the fires will overcome you and your single stream of water. The parable of serving two masters tells us that we can only fully serve one. In this case, one fire at a time.

What would a firefighter do in this situation? Call for reinforcements? Is that how you would solve the dilemma? After all, you are human, a true problem solver. What if your fire engulfs the entire city? Are there enough firefighters to take care of all the houses? Probably not. That is the problem with finite, man-driven resources; eventually they run out.

34

Focus

What if you could simply call up rain clouds and place one over every house? Why wouldn't you just do that? Problem solved …

So many times, in the middle of a firestorm at home or at work, my dreams took me to those rain clouds; hoping they would drown my current problem. It took me most of my life to understand that was NOT my job. Instead of focusing on the solution rattling around in my brain, God has led me to give ALL to Him. Big, little and everything in between. There is nothing too big or too small for God. Scripture directs us to give it all to the one who created it all.

While we have no understanding of how to single-handedly, put out two fires at the same time, God does!

> "WHEN TROUBLE COMES,
> FOCUS ON GOD'S ABILITY
> TO CARE FOR YOU."
>
> Charles Stanley

LOVE GOD FIRST BY:

"Putting Your focus only on God!."

GRATITUDE

GIVE THANKS IN ALL THAT YOU DO!

CHAPTER 3

"MAKE THANKFULNESS
YOUR SACRIFICE TO GOD ...."
PSALM 50:14 NLT

What Guides Your Relationship with God?

Don't we all enjoy being appreciated? If you are like me, those two simple words: *thank you*, always bring joy. Scripture tells us we are made in the image of God. So, "*thank you*" must bring God joy as well. Is that so hard to grasp?

Can you see God smiling?

God is joyful and like any father, He wants us to be happy and joyful as well. In my experience one of the best ways to bring joy is a simple, heart-felt "*thank you*" to friends, loved ones, and more importantly, God.

Leaving school at the age of seventeen, it seemed my life would not match my dreams. Getting a job in a dirty warehouse in Des Moines, Iowa, there was not even a glimmer of thought that someday there would be a patent in my name. Marrying the love of my life at twenty years old was the best thing that has ever happened to me. The time with my new bride seemed to wash away so much pain and doubt in those early, uncertain years. Spending every day with my favorite person made our life together so easy. Most of our days together have been full of joy and peace. We have had a great life and are blessed with four of the best kids anyone could

> "IF THE ONLY PRAYER YOU SAY
> THROUGHOUT YOUR LIFE
> IS "THANK YOU," THEN THAT
> WILL BE ENOUGH."
>
> Elie Wiesel, Holocaust survivor

hope for. My career took me away from home a lot, so most of the time my bride would stay at home to ensure the kids always had someone there to love and guide them. Thank God that she was their mother, and my beautiful bride.

My dad taught me to never say 'no' to an opportunity that would improve our lives. Following Dad's guidance took us all over the country. By the time our oldest son was eighteen, he had lived in seventeen houses. Starting in Iowa, my career took us to Texas, then Washington D.C. From DC we went to Pennsylvania and then New Jersey. Wanting to raise our kids closer to family took us back to Minneapolis, and after a few years, God led us to Arizona, where we have been for the last twenty years. All the while, when it was time to change jobs, my beautiful bride would pack up the house and the kids and follow my career with me. The multitude of jobs became my education, a master's degree from the University of Hard Knocks. Good Ol' UHK, my alma mater.

From the beginning, my heart was filled with gratitude. Always taking time to pinch myself and say thanks to God for bringing us through the many struggles and deliver our family into prosperity. It was commonplace to go through some "end of the world" struggles with money, jobs or relationships only to be immensely blessed with God's favor shortly after. The more thankful we were, the more favor came our way.

> Be anxious for nothing, but in everything by prayer and supplication with thanksgiving let your requests be made known to God.
>
> Philippians 4:6

One of my fondest memories was when we accepted the position that took us from Iowa to Texas. We were so broke that we couldn't even pay attention! Then the offer of a dream job for me came up: to open an office in Dallas for a startup technology company. The problem was, there was no money to get there. Even if we made the trek from Iowa to Texas, we didn't own a car that would allow me to do my job. It seemed my dream job was just that. A dream. My memory is vague on how we got to Texas, except for flashbacks of U-hauls, my wife, three kids, my brother, his wife, and their son traversing through a torrent of Midwestern thunderstorms for what seemed like weeks of travel.

The car problem had been solved by my kind and loving father-in-law. He had recently acquired his dream car. A beautiful 1974 bright red Grand Torino Elite in perfect condition.

White leather seats, moon roof and every accessory available. You could see how much he loved that car by the gleam in his eyes every time he would drive it. He babied that car like a proud papa with an infant son. Finding out about our predicament, he handed us the keys to his prized possession and told us to pay him back when we could. That simple blessing was the spark that ignited my career, leading to my education at UHK.

One day, driving down a Texas highway, staring at the windshield, my eyes welled up in gratitude. Gratitude to my loving father-in-law and overflowing joyous gratitude to God for delivering us to this new career; putting us on the road to success. The emotions were overwhelming, creating an intense desire to pull off the road and cry my eyes out in overwhelming thankfulness.

> "THANK YOU, GOD, FOR THIS GOOD LIFE AND FORGIVE US IF WE DO NOT LOVE IT ENOUGH."
>
> Garrison Keillor

My career exploded beginning in Texas. This high school dropout had been thrust into the world of publishing by working at a technology company that disrupted the industry with something called "Desktop Publishing." The idea that *professional production typesetting* and *publishing* could be done on an inexpensive personal computer (PC) was akin to telling Mario Andretti that a VW Bug could win the Indy 500. It was viewed by most as next to impossible.

This turned out to be one of my favorite jobs. It was this job and experience, teaching the world that a VW can, in fact, win the Indy 500 that God used to teach me perseverance, believing in myself while disregarding the pessimists. In just a few short years, most of the magazines and periodicals in the USA were being produced on software by this startup on a PC. From *Condè Nast* and *Cahner's* publications, to *Playboy* and even the *Sears* catalog; all published entirely on PC's. Emboldened by my experiences, it became clear to me that anything dreamt could be accomplished. All it took was a little extra work, some time away from family, and most importantly, gratitude to God.

God laid groundwork in me that didn't seem like training back in the day. While the professors at good ol' UHK were taskmasters, the friction of "on the job training" strengthened me like iron fortified in a furnace. In my experience, God gives us talent and capabilities that might seem small and trivial to most. However, it is these small quirks that make us unique, how we are made, God's design for our life. Often, it is our differences that set us apart from others. When viewed positively and with gratitude, what so many see as failings or weaknesses are often transformed into our best strengths.

> Let us come before His presence with thanksgiving, Let us shout joyfully to Him with psalms.
>
> **Psalm 95:2**

Let me give you an example. My love of art, and the knowledge gained through my passion for creation, has given me an understanding of balance in form, substance and color, all things that cannot be taught. My voracious consumption of TV and movies taught me so much about the art of presenting ideas, which became the foundation of most of my work in corporate presentations.

As a young boy, assisting my dad to do the "make-up" of his ads for work taught me page composition, with a mindful eye of where the reader's eyes travel and where they stop. My love of music with impactful lyrics led me to adopt princi-ples from the lyrics that still guide my life today. There truly is beauty in everything, if we just look for it. Always giving thanks to God for His favor of clarity and His glorious gift of understanding.

As my career flourished, my days became jam-packed, making time my biggest priority. My triumphs had given me a track record of success that eclipsed my lack of education. Like any achievement, it seemed critical to keep succeed-ing. The farther up the ladder, the busier my life became. The challenge with abundant success is that it takes a lot of time. Eventually there was little time to be thankful or time to spend with God.

> "GOD GAVE YOU A GIFT OF
> 86,400 SECONDS TODAY.
> HAVE YOU USED ONE TO SAY
> 'THANK YOU?'"
>
> William A Ward

At the dawn of the new millennium, God and my career had taken me to the senior staff of a Fortune 500 company. The company had offered me a position in their corporate headquarters in Philadelphia, one of our favorite cities. The new position would task me with bringing the static, mono-lithic sales company into the present by building an "on-line" Internet presence.

With no previous experience implementing Internet technology at any level, the prospect of transforming this multi-national corporation was formidable, to say the least. Choosing to commute from Phoenix, instead of relocating, amplified the stress. Weekends in Phoenix, workdays in Philly, week after week, until the project was completed.

On the initial flight to Philly, my thoughts revolved around my inadequacies, like "What were they thinking? How would my lack of education hold me back?" Feeling like an impostor, my doubts began to consume my every thought.

Most of my *"Why Me?"* questions were answered that first Monday morning while sitting in Sara's office. Sara, my new boss, was the senior VP (Sr VP) of Marketing and was a scrapper just like me. Having recently been recruited to bring the company into the new millennium, she had clear, precise goals. She was emphatic about attaining each one, and anyone who got in the way would become casualties. Sara had recruited me out of our marketing offices in Scottsdale, quickly introducing me to the hatred and vitriol that was rampant in corporations at the beginning of the new century. She saw everyone in marketing as her soldiers, battling to get the company on track. She explained how the Sr VP in charge of information technology systems (IT), and our marketing group, were embroiled in a dispute over the company's Internet public presence. The IT division had just come through all the hoopla associated with the year 2000 (Y2K) bug at the turn of the century. As the new corporate saviors, they were flexing their muscle by acquiring responsibility for as much corporate turf as they could grab. The Sr VP of IT was taking on and annihilating everyone in his path. Until Sara. Talking with Sara that first day in her office, she made my job description very clear. No discussion about marketing or strategic planning; her directive was simple. *"Take that SOB out!"* Full of the passion and fire that she was notorious for, Sara went on, *"Marketing owns the Internet, not IT! Your job is to stop them at ALL costs."* Gone were any ambiguous

> That I may proclaim with the voice of thanksgiving And declare all Your wonders.
>
> **Psalm 26:7**

wondering of what my job was. Without a doubt, we were at war. Not really the job description we had talked about in my interview.

That's how the year started, anxiously going to war with an entrenched division of people and technology capable of striking down my initiatives at every turn. Such was my introduction to Fortune 500 corporate politics. Gone were the collaborations of my past. Now it was all about alliances, budget and resources. Stories and PowerPoints were no longer

> "I WENT TO SLEEP LAST NIGHT
> AND I AROSE WITH THE DAWN,
> I KNOW THAT THERE ARE OTHERS
> WHO'RE STILL SLEEPING ON,
> THEY'VE GONE AWAY,
> YOU'VE LET ME STAY,
> I WANT TO THANK YOU.
> "THANK YOU, LORD"
>
> Maya Angelou

my weapons of choice. All my battles were now fought with spreadsheets and reports. Much like a Calvary soldier being relegated to fight in the infantry, the battlegrounds and weapons were as foreign to me as a cannon would have been to Sitting Bull.

Our claim was simple, if it touches the customer in any way, it belongs to Marketing, not IT. Thankfully, in the end, our CEO agreed. However, it took an entire year to get to that agreement. A year that, for me, was the worst year of my career. Every Sunday you could find me flying all the way across the country to start fresh every Monday morning in the throes of war. Up to, and until that point, my belief in God and "unconditional love" had carried me through most situations, good and bad. Now caught in the furnace of corporate politics, my resolve to love others was tested every part of every day. Getting on that plane on Sundays was not fun. In contrast, coming home on Friday was cause for celebration.

Nearing the end of my 12-month commitment, on a cold Philadelphia Friday morning, driving from the hotel to work into a bright and beautiful sunrise full of reds, blues and oranges was cause for reflection. The site was breathtaking, and the colors looked like they escaped from Monet's brush. The intense new-day sun was splitting the horizon through a shelf of dark purple clouds.

Blinded by the light, my thoughts went to my father-in-law's favorite nautical weather forecast. "Red sky at night, sailors' delight. Red sky at morning, sailors take warning." Now, is this a warning? What did the sunset look like last night? Pulling into the parking lot, my thoughts were quickly flooded with the anxiety of stepping into battle for the

> Enter His gates with thanksgiving And His courts with praise. Give thanks to Him, bless His name.
>
> Psalm 100:4

next eight hours. However, for now, sitting down at my desk brought a grin to my face, lifting my cheeks with thoughts of going home in a few short hours.

Gratefully, my anxious days were dwindling with every turn of the calendar. My father-in-law's adage was a distant thought, until looking out and seeing the rain on the windows while sitting down for lunch in the cafeteria.

Philadelphia weather could be fickle. Technically inland, the proximity to the Atlantic Ocean could bring severe weather from the latest Nor'easter, or intense winds from remnants of a dissipating hurricane. Today, what looked like a gentle winter rain quickly morphed into an ice storm. Looking outside after lunch everything was coated in a shiny glaze of ice, making the Valley Forge office park look more like Neverland than the headquarters of a multinational Fortune 500 corporation.

Back in my office, a quick check at my computer brought a smile, seeing Phoenix was a balmy 70°, with nothing but sunshine in the forecast for the "The Valley of the Sun!"

The great thing about the commute home was traveling west through three time zones, my plane would land close to the time of my departure from the east coast. This day couldn't be over soon enough.

> ## "WHY SHOULD WE GIVE GOD THANKS? BECAUSE EVERYTHING WE HAVE COMES FROM GOD."
>
> Billy Graham

After another day full of arguments and meetings, the clock in the board room finally clicked on 4 p.m. Grabbing my stuff, at last it was time to jump in the rental car and head for the airport to catch my 8:00 p.m. flight!

Walking outside, the icy wonderland - once pristine - was now covered in a thick blanket of sticky wet snow. Barely able to see across the parking lot through the blinding flakes of falling snow, the trek became cumbersome; unable to tell one vehicle from another because of the 2 inches of snow piled neatly on each car, the search seemed futile. Finally, pulling out my key fob to honk the horn got me to the right snow pile on four wheels. Once everything was brushed off, it was clear that the doors and windows were sealed in thick ice.

Growing up in Iowa gave me a good understanding of how to dig a car out of the worst winter storms. Unfortunately, my rental was missing the essential ice scraper or snow brush. The 10° sunset left me only the car heater and my credit cards to scrape away all the ice and snow. Actually, pulling out of the parking spot occurred almost an hour after finding my car; still very thankful, though, because there were still a few hours before my plane left for Phoenix.

Snarled was an understatement for traffic heading down I-495 to the airport. This mess brought back all those memories in Iowa of car after car spinning into a ditch full of snow. With little to no traction, the interstate was now slicker than a hockey rink that had just been Zambonied. The 10-mph procession to the airport was exhausting. The drive that was typically a quick twenty minutes took more than two hours. Still thankful, you could see me walking up to the ticket counter, learning that there was still an hour before my flight, and feeling lucky to be there.

> but thanks be to God, who gives us the victory through our Lord Jesus Christ.
> 1 Corinthians 15:57

Thankful was not the expression on the faces of my fellow travelers standing in line. Each one expressing intense anxiety in their own unique way. Without a word, each face told a story of personal distress.

Just then, the crackle of the PA announced, "*Flight 1955 to Phoenix has been canceled,*" followed by a collective sigh of extreme frustration.

The once passive and quiet line of frustrated travelers now erupted into chaos and bedlam. Gone was all civility, beginning with snide comments and grumbling being hurled at the two ticket agents working to process the crowd with haste. It seemed all rationale had been tossed aside and vitriol was rampant with every person in line, each one demanding that the airline get them home. **Tonight!**

Sadly, my attitude wasn't much better. Taking all my frustration out on the frail, elderly lady on the other side of the counter, in my loudest voice, using words that hadn't crossed my lips for decades; letting this sweet soul know my deepest frustration. Anger that probably had more to do with my war with the Sr. VP of IT and the storm, than somebody's grandmother helping me with tickets.

> "IF GOD HAS MADE YOUR CUP
> SWEET, DRINK IT WITH GRACE.
> IF HE HAS MADE IT BITTER,
> DRINK IT IN COMMUNION
> WITH HIM."
>
> Oswald Chambers

Well, my loud bullying seemed to work. With frail fingers typing as fast as possible, she found a flight that was still planning to leave and booked me on it. Without even a grumpy thank you, others witnessed me grabbing the tickets out of her hand and running to catch the plane before anyone could stop me.

At this point it was now a quest to get on that plane, any plane. Looking at my ticket my new plane was boarding in fifteen minutes at gate A 22. Standing in D Terminal at gate 24, it couldn't have been farther away. Off on a slow trot, like the Pony Express, nothing would deter me from my destination and the warmth of the Phoenix sun.

Arriving at the gate, sweat pouring off my face, it was so great to see people getting on a plane. Gone were any concerns over seat assignment, just as long as my feet stepped into the plane. The plane was jammed with bodies and winter travel gear, with barely enough room to walk down the narrow aisle to the back of the plane. Making my way to the second to the last row, there it was, the seat that would soon be taking me to warmth. No thoughts were given to it being a "middle" seat, nor that there were two very large bearded guys on either side: just plopping into it for the ride back home was enough to feel it was "mission accomplished!"

A few minutes passed as more passengers found their way to a seat. There was patience in the knowledge that soon we would be in Charlotte on our first leg of the journey. Looking at my ticket, it was now obvious the miracle that the frail ticket agent had accomplished. While the usual five-hour trip would now take nine hours; with stops in Charlotte, Houston and Dallas, it would land in Phoenix in time to take my bride out for Saturday breakfast. A feeling of triumph and warm calm swept over me like feeling the Phoenix sun on my face.

> Let the peace of Christ rule in your hearts, to which indeed you were called in one body; and be thankful.
>
> Colossians 3:15

The Captain introduced himself over the PA, increasing my joy with the inevitable departure comments. But like popping a balloon on my birthday, he then said... *"Our sincere apologies folks, looks like this storm is bigger and stronger than anyone thought. They just informed us that all flights have been canceled, and they are closing the airport until morning."*

GRATITUDE

If you know airplane travel, you know the worst thing that can happen is a canceled flight with the closing of the airport. The only thing worse is to be sitting in the back of the plane when it's canceled.

After what felt like hours, my shuffled steps got me to the front and off the plane, only to find an almost closed airport. No food, only more grumpy people just like me.

Fortunately, using my cell phone while waiting to get off the plane enabled me to find a room for the night close to the airport. Getting to my room after midnight it felt almost as cold inside as it was outside. There was no food to be found anywhere, all restaurants and pizza deliveries were closed. Thankfully, the front desk was well stocked with $1 dollar bills that worked in the vending machines.

> WHENEVER AN OPPORTUNITY
> COMES YOUR WAY, CHALLENGE
> YOURSELF TO FIRST THANK
> GOD AND THEN QUICKLY
> FOLLOW UP WITH THE
> QUESTION, "GOD, WHO ELSE IS
> SUPPOSED TO BE BLESSED BY
> THIS CONNECTION
> OR OPPORTUNITY?"
>
> Lysa TerKeurst

After a gourmet meal of Frito's, pretzels and potato chips, followed by a granola bar for dessert, it was time for bed at 1:00 a.m. with a wake-up call for 4:00 a.m. in order for me to catch the 5:00 a.m. airport shuttle. The airline had me scheduled on a 7:00 a.m. flight that would still get me home early Saturday morning. Rolling over to go to sleep, news of the

49

storm was all over the TV, already nicknamed the "Presidents Day Blizzard." The storm had clobbered the east coast, with frigid temperatures of 10°-15° and snowfall of up to 4 inches an hour. Before long, the phone was ringing, letting me know it was time to get up.

Peering through the window caked in ice, there were signs of life in the long van warming up to shuttle us back to the airport. If nothing else, a packed van was sure to keep me insulated for the ride. Coming from Arizona, it was not my practice to bring heavy coats, scarfs and gloves. Heading out to the van in a leather bomber jacket left me stiff and frozen, with a very bad attitude.

Devote yourselves to prayer, keeping alert in it with an attitude of thanksgiving;

Colossians 4:2

Unable to see inside the van through the steamed-over, icy, windows had me wondering about the others who were forced to take this frigid journey. Walking up to the van, the double doors flew open and a lady traveler appeared, greeting me with an exuberant and joyful, *"Mornin' brother! Climb on in, we got plenty of room!"* Looking for an open seat, the nine-passenger van was full. Counting only six faces, all smiling ear to ear, they were telling me to jump in. Squeezing in between two of the passengers made me think, "At least warmth won't be an issue."

It turned out my travel companions were all from a church in Tucson heading home from a conference. Not being very friendly after the ordeal of the last few days kept me silent. Silent and grumpy, my thoughts were filled with wondering what could happen next. Thinking the worst had me searching for that Zen-like zone to teleport me to the *Valley of the Sun*, as a way to endure the trip to the airport.

Settling into the peace and quiet of the pristine, yet frozen, morning, a loud shrill voice broke the silence. It rattled me back to reality with the words, *"Girl, he don't want to hear nuttin' from you but THANK YOU!"* Acting like the leader of the group, the lady sitting up front was "schooling" the passenger sitting all the way in the back of the van. Sounding more like a revival meeting than a shuttle van, they even broke into some gospel songs on our short trip. Normally, gospel music is one of my favorites. However, gospel was not on my playlist that frigid morning in Philadelphia.

> "THE GREATEST HONOR WE
> CAN GIVE ALMIGHTY GOD IS
> TO LIVE GLADLY BECAUSE OF
> THE KNOWLEDGE OF
> HIS LOVE."
>
> Julian of Norwich

Finally, the roar of the jet engines filled my ears, and thanks to my airline status, there was a comfortable seat in first class waiting for me to settle into for the trip home. Working to shake all the anxiety of the last couple of days, sipping on coffee from a real coffee cup, and munching on "first class" pastry was a good start. My thoughts were focused on the snowstorm, the cold hotel room, and my vending machine dinner re-igniting the anxiety and angst of my journey.

Sitting in the wide first-class seat while wallowing in my self-pity, the normal airplane drone was interrupted with a loud, yet very familiar voice from the back rows. Getting louder, the laughter now filled the plane. Wondering why the voice was so familiar, it hit me. It was her! The lady from the van. All six ladies were still deep in revival, giving all glory and praise to God. Talk about a joyful noise.

My first reaction was intolerance, wondering how they could have such disrespect for all of us on the plane. Grabbing my headphones and cranking up the music to drown out the incessant cackling helped, while still searching for that Zen-like zone to carry me back to Phoenix.

Just as the plane leveled out from its climb to the clouds with my music at full volume, there was a loud voice that bellowed through my ears above it all, saying, *"Girl, he don't want to hear nuttin' from you, but THANK YOU!"*

One quick turn to see if she was standing behind me, but she wasn't. Glancing back affirmed my suspicion. She was still with the group in joyous praise, and then it hit me: the voice was coming from inside me. Repeatedly, the voice echoed in my ears for the rest of my journey home.

giving thanks to the Father, who has qualified us to share in the inheritance of the saints in Light.

Colossians 1:12

In All Things, Give Thanks

It was that trip, at the end of the worst year of my career, that God taught me the most valuable lesson of my life. In ALL things, give thanks. Not just the good things, not just the big things, but ALL things.

From that day forward it has been my practice to say thanks to God for everything. Thankful for the blessing of abundance, thankful for stressful times, and thankful for something as simple as catching a plate before it crashes to the floor. Understanding that God sees and knows all, He knows when we are grateful and when we are grumpy. For me, it is always difficult to be grumpy while being thankful. It is in our gratitude that God washes away our grumpiness and replaces it with joy. It is a kind of joy that will make you and God smile.

GRATITUDE

Thanks be to God for putting me in that van, on a cold day in Philly, and thanks for speaking to me through that beautiful and joyous angel! Always remember, **the more thankful we are, the more of God's favor comes our way.**

"A STATE OF MIND THAT SEES
GOD IN EVERYTHING IS
EVIDENCE OF GROWTH IN GRACE
AND A THANKFUL HEART."
Charles Grandison Finney

LOVE IN ACTION

JUST SAY THANKS!

When we are deep in our self-pity, spouting one "*Oh Woe Is Me*" after another, it is difficult to say those two simple words: thank you. For me, there are times when saying thanks is the furthest thing from my mind. If my anger doesn't take over, it always seems that some cynical comment comes out of my mouth. After all, when we can belittle someone with cynicism or sarcasm, don't we feel better? It seems so many of us have nurtured a habit of tearing others down to build ourselves up.

> But thanks be to God, who always leads us in triumph in Christ, and manifests through us the sweet aroma of the knowledge of Him in every place.
>
> 2 Corinthians 2:14

By the end of my year-long commitment in Philadelphia, sarcasm and skepticism had washed away most of my positive attitude. Day after day of arguing had left me tired and frustrated. In my fatigue, it became easy to take the short cut. Often rolling from my mouth was one snide comment after another to end an argument. Sadly, my sharp, negative wit became a formidable weapon. As with most of the people embroiled in our corporate war, negative, hateful comments were used to gain points with a room full of like-minded, intolerable people. After all, if you can't beat them, join them. Right?

Scripture warns of falling victim to the temptation to join others in their hatred and vitriol. So often in my career, it was those times when my self-assured attitude controlled me, that everything in my world would come crashing down around me.

During that long flight to Phoenix, with that angel's voice ringing in my ears, God reminded me of the power of **thank you**. Being thankful is a two way street. When we say thank you to someone, what do they usually do? They smile. In everything we do in our relationships, there is always a reaction. We see it all the time. When we yell at someone, they yell back. When we whisper, all of a sudden everyone in the room is very quiet. When we say thank you, the smile we see is the result of joy. As small and short as it might be, it is always joy.

> "TO BE GRATEFUL IS TO RECOGNIZE THE LOVE OF GOD IN EVERYTHING HE HAS GIVEN US, AND HE HAS GIVEN US EVERYTHING."
>
> Thomas Merton

The blessings we find in our lives are the result of how we treat others. Sure, we all have times when we push back with anger or hate, thinking we have been defeated. Feeling like we are weak and ineffectual. It is those times the words of Jesus come to mind. *"Turn the other cheek."* How does that work? Is it gonna hurt?!

God does not promise that there will never be pain. However, He does promise that He will cover and comfort you through whatever trial you are confronted with.

Many times in my life when someone was berating me with one insult after the other, saying, *"Thank you,"* or something born of love, would take the wind out of their sails. Most times it leaves them speechless. Love is the unstoppable force of the universes.

Gratitude brings joy. Joy is a fruit of the Holy Spirit. Like all of the Fruit of the Spirit, it is a gift from God. It is when we give much, much is given to us.

In Christ, we work to grow close to God, and by His promise, He will grow close to us. Like all relationships, our bond with God is give and take. If all we do is take; it's not really a relationship. Gratitude is vital to all of our interactions with others, including God!

A simple *"thank you"* or even a smile is a gift to others. Always remember: how we treat others is how others will treat us.

LOVE GOD FIRST BY:

"Always saying, **'Thank you, God!'**

For everything, ... Big, small, good, or bad.

Everything!"

And in that day you will say,
"Give thanks to the LORD,
call on His name.
Make known His deeds
among the peoples;
Make them remember
that His name is exalted."

Isaiah 12:4

LoveOthersLoudly

SECTION

"For everything created by God is good, and nothing is to be rejected if it is received with gratitude;"

1 Timothy 4:4

Love PEOPLE GRATEFULLY!

DEVOTION
LOVE WITH COMMITMENT!

CHAPTER 4

"NEVER LET GO OF LOYALTY
AND FAITHFULNESS.
TIE THEM AROUND YOUR
NECK; WRITE THEM ON
YOUR HEART."

PROVERBS 3:3 GNT

Can We Be Devoted Without Love?

Would your friends, family, and loved ones describe you as devoted? How would you define devotion in others? Is devotion only about love, friendship, and our relationships?

Can we be devoted to someone, we haven't met?

DEVOTION

According to the dictionary, devotion is all about being loyal, faithful, true, staunch, steadfast, constant, committed, and dedicated. We can add to this the emotionally-driven devotion of someone who is loving, affectionate, caring, attentive, warm, and passionate. So, technically, a devoted person is loving with commitment. Sort of like the Boy Scouts Oath. All that's missing is being joyful. Can we be devoted without joy?

My research took me deep into the meaning of devotion, learning the root word is vow. This surprised me, yet this revelation makes perfect sense. After all, aren't our marriage vows all about love and commitment - devotion? Hopefully, with a little bit of joy sprinkled on top!

> "BUT LOVE, I'VE COME TO
> UNDERSTAND, IS MORE THAN
> THREE WORDS MUMBLED...
> BEFORE BEDTIME.
> LOVE IS SUSTAINED BY ACTION,
> A PATTERN OF DEVOTION IN
> THE THINGS WE DO FOR
> EACH OTHER EVERY DAY."
>
> Nicholas Sparks

Sadly, it seems as if commitment has been eliminated from the practice of our marriage vows, leaving only a contract that can be broken at the first sign of trouble. My bride of 45 years would probably tell you that there were plenty of troubled times that tested our marriage and our commitment. It was only our devotion (vow) to each other, and to God, that carried us through the storms.

Love PEOPLE GRATEFULLY!

When we decided to get married, it was important for both of us to agree that we were in it for the long haul. We would not be a statistic in the already-burgeoning divorce rates across America and the world. We agreed to make our marriage vows a covenant with God. The covenant made us both accountable to God, positioning Him as the ultimate arbitrator for all our impasses. When our devotion to each other would weaken at the sight of trouble, our devotion to God would give us strength to persevere. He always showed us a clear path forward.

So, it seems to me that devotion has another characteristic: Accountability. Not so much being held accountable, as just knowing that someone cares and is watching.

Throughout my career, it has been my joy and honor to work with some very devoted people. These experiences have bolstered my belief that devotion to a cause, idea, or group of people is the cornerstone of all success in business, organizations, and relationships. Without devotion, it is simply too easy to bail out and move on to something new.

> *A wicked messenger falls into adversity, But a faithful envoy brings healing.*
>
> **Proverbs 13:17**

In one of my first roles employed by a Fortune 500 Company, it was my pleasure to work with two of these devoted leaders in a small division that had recently been acquired by the global company.

These two leaders were the entrepreneurial team that built the newly-acquired company. Formerly the CEO and COO of their own business, they were now Executive Vice Presidents of the division that was created out of their former company. Like most successful acquisitions, the parent company worked hard to keep the management team together, along with most of the employees.

While now a small division in a huge company, the day-to-day operations were still very independent of the home office. The separation from the corporate offices of over two thousand miles seemed to strengthen the entrepreneurial spirit. Instead of dissolving it (as many believed might happen), the strength and resolve of these two leaders kept the division intact and growing as a mostly independent entity. Well, at least in the beginning.

> "IN MATTERS OF EQUITY
> BETWEEN MAN AND MAN,
> OUR SAVIOR HAS TAUGHT US
> TO PUT MY NEIGHBOR IN PLACE
> OF MYSELF, AND MYSELF IN
> PLACE OF MY NEIGHBOR"
>
> Isaac Watts

Growing up, when faced with an insurmountable force, my father would always say, *"Where does an elephant sit? Anywhere he wants to!"* After years of contemplation, Dad's comment always served to remind me of an elephant's sheer power and size, making me cautious of elephants in my path. Well, it wasn't long before the corporate elephant came to sit on top of our little division.

Complaining about difficulties in communication and the maverick operations of the division and its leaders, people at the top decided to shut down the operation and move everything to the corporate headquarters where it would be simpler to manage (control). Truth be known, it was more about the power of adding forty plus jobs to the Senior VP's direct reports at corporate, giving her more power and clout among her peers. Sadly, ambitious people can also be corporate elephants with power-hungry motivation.

All of us were shocked and confused, especially our two leaders. After all, we were not only meeting milestones, we were blowing them away at every step. As entrepreneurs often do, our leaders looked at the irrational decision of corporate as a huge mistake. It was. However, the bigger the elephant, the more times it seems to sit down in its own dung heap.

Our two leaders had already "cashed in" when selling the business. Both could have stood by and watched headquarters shut down the division. They were paid well for their parts of the company and the move could free them to pursue other interests. But that did not happen. Not these two. Instead, their devotion to the people who helped them build the company fueled their passion to fight back and stop the demise of the business they had all built together.

> Therefore, those also who suffer according to the will of God shall entrust their souls to a faithful Creator in doing what is right.
>
> 1 Peter 4:19

A call was made to corporate that resulted in a one-shot attempt to present our case to the powers that be. The next few weeks taught me so much about leadership, business, and dedication. The only word that describes the two leaders is devotion. They were clearly driven by their love and commitment for a group of employees who had worked together as a team, elbow-to-elbow, to build the company. Quietly, everyone in the company watched anxiously as the management team sequestered themselves in a conference room and worked day after day until the corporate heads showed up to render their decision. A decision that, quite frankly, had probably already been made.

Prior to the day of decision, the time in the conference room (9-5 every day for weeks) was spent analyzing, arguing, dreaming, and planning. One PowerPoint after another, spreadsheets stacked to the ceiling exposing every miniscule aspect of past, present, and projected business. Each night the team would go home, say hi to their family, eat dinner, and then jump right back into detailed planning for the discussion the next day.

> "PEOPLE, EVEN MORE THAN
> THINGS, HAVE TO BE
> RESTORED, RENEWED,
> REVIVED, RECLAIMED,
> AND REDEEMED;
> NEVER THROW OUT ANYONE."
>
> Audrey Hepburn

Looking back, it, makes me think of what it must have been like to be in the "War Room" with Patton or Churchill. Our leaders' passion and devotion drove all of us to deliver our absolute best.

Well, we won. Not a timid victory; rather, a victory that is still talked about today. This little group of entrepreneurs took on the Multi-Billion Dollar Elephant. Standing under the looming shadow of that huge pachyderm's posterior we shouted … ***You Can't Sit Here!***

Love PEOPLE GRATEFULLY!

An unexpected result from the weeks in the conference room was the unshakable unity and resolve of the management team. Armed with all the knowledge and understanding forged in the planning sessions, our team had the facts and were overflowing with passion full of devotion to push back any doubts or argument.

This victory was realized not through knowledge, strength or power. It was won only by sheer devotion. Devotion of the loving leaders and the devotion of the people working with them.

"But store up for yourselves
treasures in heaven, where neither moth
nor rust destroys, and where thieves
do not break in or steal;
for where your treasure is,
there your heart will be also. ..."

Matthew 6:20-21

"FAITHFUL SERVANTS NEVER
RETIRE. YOU CAN RETIRE
FROM YOUR CAREER, BUT YOU
WILL NEVER RETIRE FROM
SERVING GOD."

Rick Warren

LOVE IN ACTION

AS YOU SOW, SO SHALL YOU REAP

So much of what a company or organization accomplishes is the direct result of their leaders and, more importantly, how they treat those in their charge. Do you sometimes feel like the boss doesn't even know who you are? How can we be loyal to someone who is unaware of who we are and what we do? Feeling invisible in the eyes of management is a lonely and often scary place.

In my early years, with no formal education, my embarrassment led me to be as invisible as possible. After all, if they didn't see me, they wouldn't think bad of me. Sadly, they also wouldn't

> Love one another warmly as Christians and be eager to show respect for one another.
>
> **Romans 12:10 GNT**

think good things about me either. After several years in management and learning that when it came time for cutbacks, most of my peers would pick people they didn't know. This realization led me to strive to be visible over transparent. Even though people knew me, there was still no commitment or devotion. It continually made me feel like a school kid that would never get picked for a team; always knowing my value for their team and confused about how and why they couldn't see my obvious athletic prowess.

Starting in management it became clear that the most important aspect of all relationships was devotion. Devotion to my team, and theirs for me. It took me awhile to grasp where devotion came from. It didn't happen my first day as a manager. Instead, those first few months were usually filled with mostly skepticism and distrust in how this guy got that job. It was little steps over time that built a base of trust and devotion. The big eye-opener came with the understanding that in order to receive devotion and commitment, my team needed to see me devoted and committed to them. They were always watching. Like my bride always reminds me, "It's caught, not taught."

In my experience, the strongest devotion came from some small actions on my part. For example, when the gossip mill would ramp up about this boss or that guy, it was always

> "THE FIRST QUESTION WHICH THE PRIEST AND THE LEVITE ASKED WAS: 'IF I STOP TO HELP THIS MAN, WHAT WILL HAPPEN TO ME?' BUT...THE GOOD SAMARITAN REVERSED THE QUESTION: 'IF I DO NOT STOP TO HELP THIS MAN, WHAT WILL HAPPEN TO HIM?"
>
> Dr. Martin Luther King Jr.

my intention to respond with a positive statement about the victim of the latest water cooler chatter. Several times, many years later, those victims would comment about how they knew what was said.

In thanking me for my support, it was clear that they would jump in a foxhole with me anytime; always making me wonder, how many times did they have my back at the water cooler?

The practice of building devotion and commitment is well covered in scripture, including: "… for whatsoever a man soweth, that shall he also reap." Galatians 6:7. This understanding led me to practice giving and acting with others in mind first. To get devotion, give devotion, to get trust, give trust and to get respect, give respect. It's just that simple.

LOVE PEOPLE GRATEFULLY BY:

*"Treating others with loving devotion,
the same way you want to be treated."*

"YOUR DEVOTION TO GOD IS ILLUSTRATED, DEMONSTRATED, AND AUTHENTICATED BY YOUR LOVE FOR OTHERS. ..."

Andy Stanley

ENCOURAGEMENT

BE NICE TO PEOPLE ON THE WAY UP
(YOU MIGHT SEE THEM ON THE WAY BACK DOWN)

CHAPTER 5

> "THIS IS WHY YOU
> MUST ENCOURAGE
> AND HELP EACH
> OTHER, JUST AS YOU
> ARE ALREADY DOING."
> 1 THESSALONIANS 5:11 CEV

Can We Climb to the Top by Lifting Others Up?

Who doesn't want to be encouraged? From the first time our parents coax us to smile as infants, to getting that compliment from a teacher in front of the class, or our first accolade at work...

Doesn't praise always make you feel good?

72

ENCOURAGEMENT

The feeling we get from praise and encouragement is contagious. As humans, we're wired to feel good when praised. The hormone, oxytocin, sometimes called the "the love hormone," not only makes us feel great when we are praised and full of oxytocin, but the levels of oxytocin in others goes up with us and they feel great, too. Think of all those award shows and graduations you've attended. If you or a loved one was praised, how did it make you feel?

My dad always taught us that when we stop giving, we stop getting. This was his version of as you sow, so you reap. When we praise and encourage others honestly, they are moved to praise and encourage others as well. It's contagious. God's agape love version of "pay it forward" has its roots in praise and encouragement.

> "THE BEST WAY TO INSPIRE PEOPLE TO SUPERIOR PERFORMANCE IS TO CONVINCE THEM BY EVERYTHING YOU DO AND BY YOUR EVERYDAY ATTITUDE THAT YOU ARE WHOLEHEARTEDLY SUPPORTING THEM."
>
> Harold Geneen

Finding out that encouragement was an "act of love" that could only be given to others, and not ourselves, has always led me to be an encourager. Not with the intent of receiving encouragement myself; my reward was seeing the joy pouring out of someone who had just been praised.

Without a formal education, my life has been abundantly blessed in many, many ways, even without a "sheepskin" hanging on my wall. The abundance of blessings included numerous mentors who believed in me and shared with me things that weren't taught in school.

At the ripe old age of nineteen, my life was not like my friends who were still struggling with finals, girls, and part-time jobs. Instead, due to the trust of my first mentor, Mike, my life was exploding with opportunity and prosperity. On a personal level, God blessed me with the love of my life, who has been my bride now for over 45 years.

Working in a warehouse job after dropping out of school, except for meeting my soon-to-be bride, my prospects seemed bleak. That is, until the day Mike came into my life.

Mike was the classic '50-'60's-era type salesman who worked hard and smart all of his life in the music (record) business. You know, records - what people call "vinyl" today. When we first met, Mike was the national sales manager for a fledgling music distribution company working to disrupt the industry. In the early 1970's this little company had the foresight to implement computer-based stock control for automated re-ordering of inventory. Clearly, their vision was genius. Think Amazon-level controls in the 1970's! Well, their business exploded, with Mike at the helm of the sales force.

We should keep on encouraging each other to be thoughtful and to do helpful things.
Hebrews 10:24 CEV

ENCOURAGEMENT

In those days, Mike was always out walking around in the warehouse. It seemed when he wasn't traveling, he was on the frontlines with the people doing the work. Not only in the front office. That's how we got to know each other. He always impressed me with the genuine interest that he showed in the people working "in the back." Mike seemed to take a liking to me, especially when he learned about my love of music.

It really shocked him one day when our conversation turned to my appreciation of classic musicals, especially, "The Music Man," which was Mike's favorite. Telling him how the movie had inspired me to play trombone, he shouted enthusiastically, *"That record paid for my first convertible!"* From that point forward, we were buddies. An event, and friendship, that would wonderfully bless my life.

> "OUR CHIEF WANT IS SOMEONE
> WHO WILL INSPIRE US TO BE
> WHAT WE KNOW WE COULD BE."
>
> Ralph Waldo Emerson

One day Mike called me into his office. Thinking the worst, my mind went through a detailed recollection of anything that might jeopardize my job. Nothing came to mind.

Mike always had a good poker face; however, this time there was the crack of a smile coming through as he said, *"Do you like working here?"*

Well, that didn't help my anxiety. *"Yes,"* almost whispering with a subtle trembling in my voice. He continued, *"We have done an extensive evaluation of you."*

My lips must have been quivering, but that crooked smile on his face had me puzzled. Could he really enjoy firing someone this much?

Mike went on to say, *"With your work ethic and obvious love for music, we believe you would make an excellent sales representative for our company."*

His smile was now ear to ear as he went on to say, *"We have an opening in our Western territory and would like to offer you the position."*

The feelings that exploded inside of me were intense. To look at me, you would have seen a young man struggling to act like a grown up, biting

> You obey the law of Christ when you offer each other a helping hand.
> Galatians 6:2 CEV

my lip and doing everything possible not to cry. Mike's belief and trust were one of the kindest things anyone has ever done for me. The feeling was amazing.

Just think, while most of my friends were still going to school; this 19-year-old high school dropout was about to get a company car, an expense account, and a decent salary. No more punching a time clock!

And the most wonderful thing about it was that Mike trusted me. He trusted me to represent a multi-million-dollar company, and he trusted me to get the job done. Trusted by not only the muckety-mucks high up in the company; but more importantly, trusted by Mike.

ENCOURAGEMENT

My relationship with Mike quickly morphed from casual friend to mentor-protégé. He took me under his wing, teaching me the core of my business acumen. He taught me the rules of etiquette like what to order for breakfast, and how to dine with customers, as well as complex things like how to read a spreadsheet. Through his patience and kindness, Mike taught me things no one else could have. Today, most of my business knowledge can be traced back to lessons learned from Mike. He was not only that good of a teacher, but his unconditional love established my approach to relationships for the rest of my life.

> "EVERYONE HAS INSIDE THEM A PIECE OF GOOD NEWS. THE GOOD NEWS IS YOU DON'T KNOW HOW GREAT YOU CAN BE! HOW MUCH YOU CAN LOVE! WHAT YOU CAN ACCOMPLISH! AND WHAT YOUR POTENTIAL IS."
>
> Anne Frank

One of the many lessons that Mike taught me paved the way for so many great relationships as a mentor, and as a protégé. One day, as we were calling on a giant discount retailer, Mike led me right past the office and all the way back to the warehouse at the very end of the building.

On our way he said, *"Always remember to get to know the people in the back, as well as, if not better than, the people in the front office. From time to time you'll need their help. And, in my experience, they will rarely let you down."*

Looking back, that simple statement guided the steps of my career. From that day forward, most of my time was spent in the warehouses of my customers instead of their front office. Often it made me think of Mike. Albeit, Mike probably would have told me to focus on the task and quit my daydreaming.

One day, several years after working with Mike, God and my career led me to a small technology company in Minneapolis while my wife and kids stayed on the east coast to finish out the school year. The company had a phenomenal plan for promotion through self-education on their products. With my family so far away, there was ample time at night to work on the training. As a result, night after night you would find me alone in the office, "schooling" myself.

One night, a recruit named Vince showed up. Looking like a direct descendant of Paul Bunyan, this burly guy from the woods of Northern Minnesota had no clue about computers – nor technology. He just needed a job to provide for his own growing family.

"Let your light shine before men in such a way that they may see your good works, and glorify your Father who is in heaven.
Matthew 5:16

My first reaction to Vince was to ignore him. Maybe he'd just go away, taking his many hunting stories with him. However, Mike's "people in the back" lesson kept gnawing at me like one of Vince's bear stories. After a while, the two of us began having nightly meetings. His goal? Learn enough to pass the employment test, and my goal was to teach Vince as much about computers and technology as possible.

We both passed our tests and went our separate ways. For me, my career with the company blossomed. It seemed that almost instantly, my wife and family joined me in our new house, and the company had moved me into a management role. With all that was happening, Vince was not on my radar screen; other than an occasional lunchroom encounter, our paths rarely crossed.

As the years passed, the company promoted me to the position of Regional Sales Manager with an inside sales team of ten to twelve reps. Working to hit our sales quota every month kept me focused on my territory on the east coast. Vince worked in the west, so we rarely saw each other. While we both went to work in Minneapolis, we now worked in different time zones.

> ## "NO ONE IS USELESS IN THIS WORLD WHO LIGHTENS THE BURDENS OF ANOTHER."
>
> Charles Dickens

One day, my boss asked me to change territories. The west coast was in turmoil and sales were plummeting. At the core of the turmoil? You guessed it. Vince.

Starting my new position, my number one job was to get rid of Vince! In talking with everyone from the president of the company to the sales reps on the floor, they all said the same thing: Get rid of Vince!

From the stories that the team told me, Vince was intimidating everyone in the company. That is, everyone but me. He always treated me with exceptional respect. Those days working late together in the beginning set an early relationship based on trust. It was that trust that led me to talk with Vince, and not just let him go.

There we sat, eyeball to eyeball. My goal was to understand what was going on with my friend and protégé; knowing that he was better than what people were telling me. We started our meeting with me asking him to envision my hand around his neck and holding him over a deep abyss. He looked at me with terror in his eyes.

Then, looking Vince square in the eyes asking …

"Do you want me to let you go?"

"Everyone in this building wants me to let you go."

"What do you want me to do, Vince?"

He responded with stories of mistreatment and verbal abuse. Then almost begging, he told me how much he needed the job.

Building on our bond of trust, together we worked out a plan for him to stay. He was to build a territory in the Canadian territories that had never bought a single product from the company.

> *"But exhort one another every day, as long as it is called "today," that none of you may be hardened by the deceitfulness of sin."*
> Hebrews 3:13

In my experience, when people are put on a performance plan, they usually take the time to find a new job. Occasionally, they hunker down and get back on track. That is what Vince did. Within a year, that territory was consistently in the running for the number one territory in the region. Kudos to Vince for persevering. By that time, most had forgotten the chaos. Funny what success can do to bad memories.

ENCOURAGEMENT

Vince is just one of the many blessings throughout my corporate life resulting from mentor/protégé relationships. Christ teaches us to Love One Another; front office, warehouse, or street corner. No matter if you are on your way up, or going down, leading with Love will always make the ride smoother. When you focus on helping others succeed, you can't help but to succeed as well.

"INSTRUCTION DOES MUCH,
BUT ENCOURAGEMENT
EVERYTHING."

Johann Wolfgang von Goethe

Love PEOPLE GRATEFULLY!

Love In ACTION

Give a Hand, Take a Hand

Have you ever felt embarrassed in front of a crowd? Does the idea of everyone watching give you anxiety? For me, being alone in a stressful situation is about the worst thing to go through. Feeling the stares of a crowd watching my every move seems to slow down time and take control over every part of my body. How about you? Do you know the terror of being alone, especially in a crowd?

Spending most of my life on the outside looking in always made me feel inadequate. Everyone around me seemed to have great lives, full of fun, love, and friends. It always made me wonder, "What do they have that eludes me?" Over time, some became good friends of mine. To my surprise, they would tell me how they felt just as inadequate as me. How could that be? In my eyes they were living the perfect life.

> *A new commandment I give to you, that you love one another, even as I have loved you, that you also love one another.
>
> John 13:34

So many of my "perfect" friends relayed stories of having anxiety and doubt in their lives, often detailing experiences that would have devasted me. Still, they beam with confidence, clarity, and assurance. It took me a long time to understand their "secret sauce." In one word, it was encouragement. They had people in their lives that not only loved them, but throughout their lives would consistently praise, encourage, and support them.

82

ENCOURAGEMENT

Even as kids, it was easy to see encouragement all around them, from the sports trophies on the bedroom shelves, the certificates hanging on their walls, and the loving faces in pictures of the latest school concert or play. All tangible reminders of encouragement and love. Like the cliché says, someone "had their back." Was it really that simple? Could the knowledge that someone cared truly foster confidence?

Growing up, my family was fragmented by the ravages of alcoholism. For those who have experienced living in that world, you know the isolation and shame it brings. As a kid not knowing much about anything, it seemed to be normal that my parents weren't at my school events. They always seemed to have a good excuse. While my mom did a stint as our cub scout leader, she would rarely leave home. So, cub scout award ceremonies were few and far between. My

> "MINISTRY NEED NOT BE AN OFFICE; IT'S A LIFESTYLE DEVOTED TO ATTRACTING THE LOST TO CHRIST AND ENCOURAGING OTHER BELIEVERS IN THE FAITH."
>
> D.L. Moody

bedroom shelves were barren of trophies and awards except for that one golden statue from the year we won the little league championship. My one "claim to fame."

That was the year that my dad found time to coach our team. It is one of my fondest memories. Even though most of the season is a blur, lost in the brain of a nine-year-old boy, the last moments of our championship game are as clear to me now as the day it happened.

Like all great baseball stories ... it was the bottom of the ninth and the other team had just scored what could've been the winning run. We were at bat with our best hitter up first and me on deck. As he had done all year, the first batter hit the first ball thrown for a double. Now it was up to me. Talk about fear and anxiety!

Walking up to the plate and mimicking all the Mickey Mantle moves, knocking the dust off my shoes with the bat just like Mickey. Standing at the plate trying to stop my hands from shaking and my knees from wobbling as the pitcher began his warmup, my dad's bellowing voice stopped everything with a loud, "Time Out!"

My dad always had a flair for drama, this time was no different. Walking up to home plate with a grin that told me this was a tease, he asked, *"How's it going Willy?"* (Dad always called me Willy, when he was being affectionate) He went on to ask what my plan was while acting extremely serious, even though the grin never left his eyes. He then asked me to take a shot at bunting instead of hitting the ball. *"The pitcher is just as shook up as you are. He knows the game is on the line and he is not expecting a bunt."* Patting me on the back, he reassured me that he had confidence in me, and it couldn't be any better than to have me at the plate. Ending our talk with a quiet *"well-that-should-shake-up-the-pitcher"* wink and a smile, he headed back to the dugout.

> Love each other as brothers and sisters and honor others more than you do yourself.
> Romans 12:10 CEV

84

ENCOURAGEMENT

You probably have already guessed what happened. The bunt worked and the pitcher flubbed the ball, hastily trying to throw me out at second base, the ball sailed all the way out to the centerfield fence. Rounding third base and knowing we would win with my score; the excitement was incredible. Then, there he was, my dad, standing on the other side of home plate with a huge smile and arms ready to catch me. Bouncing off home plate and into his arms is one of my best memories. Both of us crying, his words still ring in my ear … *"I knew you could do it, Willy!"*

It was his encouragement and love that carried me through my fear that day. Knowing my dad believed in me was my "secret sauce." As the years passed and my family crumbled, that feeling of someone in my corner went away. That is, until shortly after my dad passed away at the age of forty three.

> "I'D LIKE TO BE KNOWN FOR STEPPING UP AND ENCOURAGING OTHERS TO DO THE SAME."
>
> Leigh Anne Tuohy

Swamped in sadness over losing my dad led me to my knees in prayer. That is when my best friend, Christ Jesus, put His arm around me and let me know he was always in my corner. From that day forward, my life has been filled with confidence and comfort. Now, every time my thoughts go back to that baseball field in July, my feelings explode with the joy of knowing that like my father, God's arms are wrapped around me while His still, quiet voice whispers, *"I knew you could do it!"*

LOVE PEOPLE GRATEFULLY BY:

"Encouraging Them to Be Everything
God Made Them to Be!"

And looking at them Jesus said to them, "With people this is impossible, but with God all things are possible."

Matthew 19:26

AWARENESS

THE LOVE YOU TAKE, EQUALS THE LOVE YOU MAKE

CHAPTER 6

"REMEMBER THIS SAYING,
"A FEW SEEDS MAKE
A SMALL HARVEST, BUT A
LOT OF SEEDS MAKE
A BIG HARVEST."

2 CORINTHIANS 9:6 CEV

Seek to Understand or to be Understood?

Throughout my career, there was always a huge chip on my shoulder. It went everywhere with me, and anyone who would notice it, or dare comment on it, would get an earful in response. My entrance into the corporate world was different than most.

So much so, that the theme song for most of my life was, *"I'm Not Like Everybody Else,"* by my favorite band, The Kinks.

AWARENESS

The chip on my shoulder set me apart from everyone else; making me more confident the further my career advanced. Most of my peers had acquired an achievement that eluded me. They had a high school diploma. My high school dropout chip was initially covered in shame. Then, by God's favor, my career exploded. With my new-found success, the shame of my chip transformed into pride. The farther up the corporate ladder, and the more education my peers had, the more they heard me boast about my lack of a formal education. Until God's plan introduced me to Chuck.

> "THE WHOLE IDEA OF COMPASSION IS BASED ON A KEEN AWARENESS OF THE INTERDEPENDENCE OF ALL THESE LIVING BEINGS, WHICH ARE ALL PART OF ONE ANOTHER, AND ALL INVOLVED IN ONE ANOTHER"
>
> Thomas Merton

Chuck was the CEO of a small technology company in the Graphic Arts field. With Chuck's guidance, a handful of the best scientists and engineers in the Graphic Arts community carved out a unique slice in the industry. They were the pioneers that introduced Computer Generated Graphics in film to most of the world: Built on technology originally created to produce 35mm slides for business presentations (Remember the slide carousel? - An essential tool in any business presentation before PowerPoint!).

As often happens, someone with a keen, innovative eye saw a different use for their technology. How about using the same expertise to convert computer graphics to the 16mm film used in Hollywood? Boom! Mass-market Computer-Generated Imaging (CGI) was born. The idea soon found its way to Hollywood and was used in the second *TERMINATOR* movie. If you know the movie, there were a few seconds of liquid silver used to morph the next-gen Terminator back into shape. Well this little technology company, and a very deserving engineer, won an Academy Award for that few seconds of 16mm film. Not long after the T-1000 regenerated itself, Hollywood became enamored with CGI, introducing Toy Story and a host of 100%-created CGI movies. Straight from the computer to the Silver Screen. ... and as they say, the rest is history!

My meeting with Chuck was after all the hoopla of the Academy Awards. Imagine my feelings of inadequacy walking into that unassuming office for the first time. There, inside the front door, was a huge glass display case. Almost floor to ceiling shelves, full of awards and photographs, displaying the accolades of this little company's accomplishments in the film industry, complete with a replica

> For the entire law is fulfilled in keeping this one command: "Love your neighbor as yourself."
> Galatians 5:14 NIV

of the Oscar. Other than this one impressive shrine, the company looked more like an office in a rural Iowa town, than a breakthrough tech company. Then Chuck walked out of his office.

My first thought was, *"This is Chuck?!"* Not your typical tech guru. No splash, flash, or excitement. He extended his hand for a feeble handshake with eyes that did everything they could to not look at me. For a minute, he reminded me of "Corporal LeBeau," played by Holocaust survivor Robert Clary, on the TV series Hogan's Heroes.

AWARENESS

True to his French ancestry as small in stature, Chuck was as unassuming as his office. In a faint voice fitting his disposition, he invited me in to talk.

After meeting the company's Vice President of Marketing at a trade show, Chuck agreed to interview me for a job. Recently jobless due to the failure of a startup, it was imperative for me to find work. Especially with a wife and four little mouths to feed.

While the VP told me that the interview was more of a formality than anything and that the job was mine, Chuck had other ideas. Sitting down to talk, this unpretentious man seemed overly nervous. His demeanor confused me.

"IF ONE DOES NOT UNDERSTAND A PERSON, ONE TENDS TO REGARD HIM AS A FOOL"

C.G. Jung

As the meeting progressed it became clear that Chuck had misgivings about hiring me. However, the more we talked, the easier it got, and our discourse culminated into his proud recall of the company's Academy Award triumphs. Emboldened by his success story, Chuck finally looks me in the eye, and says, *"I can't hire you."* Working to regain my composure, with images of my wife and kids bouncing around in my head, the question came out. *"Why not?"*

Chuck's retort was quick. *"Because of your lack of education."* He said it like it was an obvious answer.

Fighting the temptation to let the chip on my shoulder and its vitriol take over while tightening my jaw, the words spilled out of my mouth. *"Why? What do you mean?"*

Chuck explained to me how everyone in the company - from the receptionist to the shipping guys - had college degrees. Referring to the scientists and PhD's on staff, he quietly said,

"How could I do that to them? What would they think?"

Then his eyes widened, like he just discovered gold. *"Besides, what can you do for our company, that someone with a college degree can't do?"*

Well, with that, the chip on my shoulder took over. In a wave of arrogance, the words passed my lips like it was rehearsed. *"Well Chuck, thirty days from today, this high school dropout will have the Senior Vice President of Technology for a Multi-Billion Dollar, Fortune 500 Company sitting right here in your office. They don't teach that in college!"*

Surprisingly, he was not impressed. He got up from his desk and escorted me out the door.

On my ride home, realizing that it was time to look for something else to do, my sure thing suddenly didn't look to be quite so sure.

Do nothing from selfishness or empty conceit, but with humility of mind regard one another as more important than yourselves;

Philippians 2:3

Long story short, the VP of Marketing compelled Chuck to bring me on board, anyway. Together, without a lot of support from the boss, we reinvented the company, rocking the printing industry with technology that is still used today.

It was at that job, working with all those talented people in Chuck's company, that my chip finally found respect for the brilliance that can be nurtured and guided through academics. Some of the fondest memories of my career are those brainstorming sessions and passionate debates over technology, marketing, and strategies with all the Brainiacs.

Working toward a common vision, the VP of Marketing was my colleague, my mentor and at times a protégé. We seemed inseparable. He taught me so much about marketing strategy. Thinking of him always gives me pause to thank God for bringing him into my life. On the other hand, Chuck did all he could to avoid me. Except for giving me an office across the hall from his - albeit an office that had been converted out of a closet. While Chuck probably got a laugh seeing me in the five-foot-wide, twelve-foot-deep office, it was plenty big for me and my chip!

My relationship with Chuck was tenuous at best. Eventually, we found ourselves in a contentious discussion, resulting in me getting fired or quitting. Neither of us knows who did or said what, but it was the end of my time with Chuck.

> "WHEN PEOPLE TALK
> LISTEN COMPLETELY.
> MOST PEOPLE NEVER LISTEN."
>
> Ernest Hemingway

On that day, we were embroiled in a passionate debate over the direction of the company. My chip was full of passion and dedication to my beliefs. For once, Chuck was showing fervent passion as well.

Up to this point, we had never seen eye to eye on anything. His academic bigotry always seemed to infuriate my chip. Not this day. Chuck's passion was fueled by something different. Gone were the vague references to the significance of the educated. Spilling out of Chuck's office and into the hallway, the argument could be heard throughout the office. Now nose-to-nose, Chuck yelled in my face, *"If I make a mistake it will hurt everyone in this company!"* With that, and seeing Chuck's eyes tear up, it hit me. Chuck's passion was centered in caring for the people of his company. Money and my lack of education had nothing to do with it. Like Don Mclean sung about in "The Day the Music Died," that was the day my chip died. Walking back to my office to pack up my stuff was emotional, knowing it was the end. My head and heart were filled with sadness and disappointment. This project had been such a big part of my life, and now it would be born without me. Still, Chuck's last words bounced back and forth between my heart and my head. Never had the CEO of a company showed so much love and caring for the people in their charge. My previous discussions with Chuck always centered on how much revenue our project would bring to his company. Until now, he had never shown his strong commitment to those who worked for him.

Throughout my career, when working with owners or CEO/presidents of companies, my experience always taught me to talk with them about increased revenue or reduced expenses, nothing else.

Finally, all of you should agree and have concern and love for each other. You should also be kind and humble.
1 Peter 3:8 CEV

It was now clear to me why the two of us never "clicked," or got along. That one comment showed me a side of my former boss as a leader who was radically different. Chuck loved his employees like a father loves his family; like most fathers, he would never hurt them for money.

Looking back, that event was one of God's pivot points in my life. What seemed disastrous to me, turned out to be a powerful blessing masked in chaos, turmoil, and doubt. Like so many other times, the pain heralded God's impending Grace, Favor, and Promise to come.

From that day forward, the chip on my shoulder was no longer a badge of pride. It was just another bump in the road of my life that God used to strengthen me and my resolve. To this day, my heart overflows with thankfulness that God used my time with Chuck to knock that chip off my shoulder. Without my un-educated prejudice, it became easier for me to accept people for who they were, educated or not.

> "FOCUS LESS ON THE IMPRESSION YOU'RE MAKING ON OTHERS AND MORE ON THE IMPRESSION YOU'RE MAKING ON YOURSELF."
>
> Amy Cuddy, PhD

Building on my new recognition of seeing people for who they are had empowered me for the rest of my career. Several years later when starting a position at a classic "Silicon Valley" tech company, it was my pleasure to work with another team who impressed me as some of the smartest engineers on the planet. You know, those smartest-guys-in-the-room types. In this case, my team was filled with a couple dozen of those bright technologists, including PhDs, scientists, inventors, and a collection of engineers that Steve Jobs would envy.

Often, sitting in brainstorming sessions, my mind would wander off to my tussles with Chuck and my struggles in school, leading me to ponder how these Brainiacs endured decades in school. Over lunch they would tell me how much they enjoyed the academic environment and often talked about ambitions of teaching someday. Their appreciation and dreams were as foreign to me as my stories of growing up in

Iowa were to them. Still, our love for creation and innovation bonded us together in the universe of possibilities, which eventually led me to getting a patent for our innovation.

My time with Chuck taught me that awareness is an act of love. An act that is born in understanding and unconditional love. We are all human and most use our impressions and opinions of others to shape our beliefs, ultimately holding others accountable for thoughts they may have never had. Renowned bestselling author and social psychologist, Dr. Amy Cuddy, refers to this as "Imprinting" in her bestselling book, "PRESENCE." Simply stated, "Imprinting" is when we create a thought or belief in our head that we believe someone else thinks about us. Then we hold that person accountable for a thought or belief they never had. It is only when we take time to fully understand their beliefs or thoughts, that we can begin to truly be thoughtful or empathic with them and their situation.

In my relationship with Chuck, the chip on my shoulder was a brick wall that stood between us. A wall that was put in place by my thoughts and insecurities and not his.

> Be completely humble and gentle; be patient, bearing with one another in love.
>
> **Ephesians 4:2 NIV**

It was only when understanding Chuck's beliefs and the loving kindness that he demonstrated with extraordinary and extreme passion, that his purpose-driven motivation became crystal clear to me.

How often is our relationship with God thwarted by a brick wall that we put between us? In Christ, we let our pride, our shame, and perceived inadequacies stand as obstacles between the One who created us, and our understanding of the beautiful creation He made.

96

Like the chip on my shoulder, everything we are is God's design. It is only in our perception and self-awareness that we see strength or weakness in who we are.

Chuck's passionate caring for those in his charge, along with my shame for lacking a college degree, were viewed by both of us as our vulnerabilities and weaknesses, not strengths. All the while, these experiences were powerful assets that God designed in both of us before time began. It is only when we become aware of the strength these traits give us and no longer conceal them as vulnerabilities, are we able to tear down the walls and fully, genuinely communicate.

> "I DON'T LIKE THAT MAN.
> I MUST GET TO
> KNOW HIM BETTER."
>
> Abraham Lincoln

So, Let Go! Let God build and empower the person that He sees in you!

When we let go of the perception of our ability, and how others view us, we understand who we truly are in Christ. Letting go of all things of the world, including self-loathing, you realize that every part of your life on Earth is fueled by God's Supernatural Power.

It is in this belief we find the strength of faith that comes from a peace that passes all understanding.

LOVE PEOPLE GRATEFULLY!

LOVE In ACTION

BEWARE OF DARKNESS

So many times, it appeared others were "out to get me." Do you know the feeling? All eyes seem to be on you with that x-ray vision stare, revealing your deepest and darkest feelings. That sixth sense that the people you fear most, not only know what you are thinking, but they also know how afraid you are of them.

A lot of my life was spent in that doubt and chaos. Always looking over my shoulder to see who was next to put a knife in my back. It was bad enough during my short time in school. However, those

> Therefore encourage one another and build one another up, just as you are doing.
>
> 1 Thessalonians 5:11

childhood memories of my schooltime paranoia were minuscule in comparison to my experience in corporate politics. Throughout my early career, it seemed the bulk of my time was spent preparing for that inevitable attack that never happened, but always working to be a good Boy Scout by "being prepared." In those days, being prepared was all about outguessing my opponent and working to be "two-steps ahead of the competition." Still, it seemed the more protection placed between me and my foe, the less clear the path forward was. Not unlike turning a room into a fortress, the more windows and doors that were covered up, the darker the room.

In this case, it was giving into the shame of my vulnerabilities and my perception of my adversary's motives that were blocking the view.

Over time, it became clear that hiding in the dark room of my misperception was the worst thing to do. Covering my thought windows made it impossible to be aware of what was going on with others. And the covered windows also stopped anyone from seeing the real me. If they could see into the darkened room of my mind, they would have seen a frightened and unsure opponent, instead of the unreasonable foe conjured up by their perception of me. Likewise, the darkened windows of my perception prevented me from seeing who they really were. In most cases, they were just another frightened individual, fearing defeat just like me.

It took me decades to learn the simple principle that had been staring me in the face since my youth. Darkness is only overcome by light. As scripture tells us, love always conquers hate and darkness always succumbs to light.

> ## "I THINK THAT HATE IS A FEELING THAT CAN ONLY EXIST WHERE THERE IS NO UNDERSTANDING."
>
> Tennessee Williams

With that understanding, it became my practice to always meet hate with love and to eradicate darkness with light. Sure, it can be painful to shine light on a problem, or worse, confront someone's misconceived perception of who you are or what you believe. God never said that doing the right thing would be easy or painless. Nevertheless, that is the only way to remove the perception.

Like sunlight disinfects, opening a dialogue with others to become more aware of who they are will cleanse the imperfections of your thoughts about them. Likewise, opening yourself up and being vulnerable will let them see past the blocked windows and into the soul of who you truly are.

It is only when we become aware of others and who they are, from their perspective not ours, and they become aware of the real person we are, that a relationship can grow through truth, openness and understanding.

LOVE PEOPLE GRATEFULLY BY:

"Being Aware of Who they Truly are
Through Understanding and Empathy!"

"God has given each of you a gift from his great variety of spiritual gifts. Use them well to serve one another.

1 Peter 4:10

LOVE OTHERS LOUDLY

SECTION III

"BE KIND AND COMPASSIONATE TO ONE ANOTHER,
FORGIVING EACH OTHER, JUST AS IN CHRIST
GOD FORGAVE YOU."

Ephesians 4:32

LOVE PEOPLE WITH COMPASSION!

EMPATHY

SAVIOR OR SERVANT?

CHAPTER 7

"WHOEVER IS THE
GREATEST SHOULD
BE THE SERVANT OF
THE OTHERS."
MATHEW 23:11 CEV

Are You a Helping Hand or a Knight on a Horse?

Is there someone in your life that "smothers" you in love? That person who is willing to do anything for you, even when you don't want their help? Does it seem what they do is entirely their idea, and not always what you need? Are the things they do designed to help you, or is it more about them?

Do you find their kindness born in **selflessness** or in **selfishness?**

So often, we are sympathetic toward the people we care about, jumping on our high horse, chasing windmills born in our opinion, not reality. Like Don Quixote, slaying dragons in the windmills of our minds; acting more like a Savior than a Servant. The role of savior is way above my pay grade, and my Bible tells me that the job has been filled.

So why is it that most of us want to save people? It's simple, we care. It's part of who we are as humans. We have "built-in" receptors of one another's pain, fueling our tendency and desire to help. At the core of our need to help is an understanding of the potential pain someone might experience, our fears of suffering that pain; not the person we're trying to save, working to protect someone else from the pain that we are afraid of. Pain WE don't want to experience. That is sympathy and it is usually not helpful. How often do we hear others

> ## "MOST PEOPLE DO NOT LISTEN WITH THE INTENT TO UNDERSTAND; THEY LISTEN WITH THE INTENT TO REPLY."
>
> Stephen R. Covey,
> The 7 Habits of Highly Effective People

say they don't want our sympathy? We may believe that the statement is untruthful, born from humility, vulnerability, or shame. But is it? Or is it merely a refusal of unwanted kindness formed from a misunderstanding of their needs? How often do we hear, *"You just don't understand,"* as the follow up to someone's plea for us to butt out? Do our savior-focused ears refuse to hear the clear request for a different kind of help?

So, if we are not supposed to be a savior for those we love, how do we help? Are we supposed to just stand by and watch the train wreck? Like all things in life, the answers are found in scripture. Not just one obscure verse tucked away in a corner of the Bible. Instead, the answers are the core teachings of Christ Jesus and can be found throughout His gospel. In Christ, we know the two great commandments: Love God and Love One Another. In fact, the words "One Another" appear over one hundred times in scripture. So clearly, those who walk in Christ are to care for and help each other. If we are to truly love one another, Jesus must not want us to sit by and watch the train wreck. Wouldn't you agree?

How would you stop a train wreck? Do you have the knowledge to change the outcome? Let's say you could be instantly transported into the engine room of the train. What next? Do you know what to do? Is there a brake pedal? What controls would you use? You need to think of something fast. If not, you will become a victim, not the savior. How could that be? Simple, you lack the knowledge and understanding to do anything but crash with everyone else. Isn't understanding the key? The difference between a Savior or Servant?

> Be kind to one another, tender-hearted, forgiving each other, just as God in Christ also has forgiven you.
>
> Ephesians 4:32

Have you found that people who take the time to clearly understand your situation are the ones who are prepared to help? Instead of having sympathy and feeling sorry for you, through their understanding they have empathy. Real compassion that can only come from knowing your circumstances, feelings, and fears. They appreciate how you feel, and it touches memories of their struggles, when they felt similar distress. It is with that knowledge, and shared experiences, that we can understand and love one another.

EMPATHY

In his watershed book, *The 7 Habits of Highly Effective People*, first published in 1989; Stephen Covey enlightened the world to the power of understanding, the advantage of effective goal setting and obtaining the right perspective. In Covey's Habit #5, "Seek first to understand, then to be understood," he highlights the benefits of being empathetic. In the book, Covey suggests three factors that lead to understanding: credibility, trust, and their alignment with logic. In working to truly understand, Covey points to focusing on what someone is saying and not listening while trying to come up with our reply.

> "WHENEVER YOU ARE ABOUT TO FIND FAULT WITH SOMEONE, ASK YOURSELF THE FOLLOWING QUESTION: WHAT FAULT OF MINE MOST NEARLY RESEMBLES THE ONE I AM ABOUT TO CRITICIZE?"
>
> Marcus Aurelius "the Philosopher King"

It is only when we comprehend someone's situation from their perspective, not ours, that we can begin to help.

My kids have put up with a lot of my shenanigans through the years. If they weren't posing for "artsy" photos with their wannabe-photographer dad, they were victims of my latest self-improvement practice, usually fueled by management, sales, or motivational training at work. Such was the case one fall weekend with an impromptu Saturday meeting.

Our journey took us to my offices in a beautiful Minneapolis suburb, where we had a great "brainstorming" room, the perfect venue for creative planning. It was strategically placed in the center of the building, having no windows except for one wall of glass that gave an unrestricted, bird's-eye view of the company's sales floor. During the week, the sales floor was usually packed with over fifty reps, all hunkered over their computer screens, hands covering headsets to block out noise. Each rep selling their hearts out, one one-thousand-dollar printer at a time.

The remaining three walls in the conference room were covered from floor to ceiling in white marker board; unlimited space for bombastic originality, illustrated with multi-colored, "erasable" markers. Every wall showing the dingy history of former meetings with the residue of the un-erasable dust left behind. If you looked closely, you could see colorful outlines showing traces of landing sites from airborne erasers thrown in the passion of inspiration. Some of my favorite meetings happened in that room.

> *"Blessed are the merciful, for they shall receive mercy.*
> Matthew 5:7

On this crisp fall day, the five of us piled into our minivan for a trip to Dad's office, leaving Mom at home for some much needed "mom-time." Always looking forward to my time with the kids, these weekend excursions were a great way for me to spend some dad-time with four of my all-time favorite people.

There are only faint memories of our lunchtime gathering in that unique conference room; no one is sure what prompted the meeting, nor what nugget of daddy wisdom needed to be shared that day. However, there was one simple statement that is ingrained in my brain, and always will be one of my favorite lessons that my kids taught me.

After a lengthy verbal onslaught about working together as a family, it ended with the tired cliché, *"There is no 'I' in teamwork!"* My youngest daughter, without missing a beat, blurted out, *"Yeah, but there is a ME!"* Leaving me speechless, all the kids giggled and cackled over their silly dad.

From that day forward my view of teamwork has been viewed through cynical glasses. Maybe there was always a "me" at the heart of the calls to work together. Inevitably, most team environments seemed to have that one person working to steer the team in their direction. Usually with unquestionable good intentions, assuming the role of "savior," someone is usually at the center of the team directing traffic. After all, they believed they knew the right thing to do; and were committed to ensure the fulfillment of "their" vision.

> "HELP SOMEONE, YOU EARN A
> FRIEND. HELP SOMEONE TOO
> MUCH, YOU MAKE AN ENEMY."
>
> Erol Ozan

I Have, Me & Mine

Throughout my career there were hordes of saviors riding in to save the day. All heralding the power of teamwork and camaraderie. Each one with their own agenda and a clear benefit for their career, their bank account, or both. Few and far between were the servants: those leaders who were truly focused on eliminating problems with no regard for personal rewards or gain.

Participating in many failed resurrections by saviors, and the chaos that ensued, it became easier to identify the saviors or "white knights" as they were riding in. In contrast, servants were so rare, they stood out like beacons of warm sunshine wherever they were.

When the latest savior arrived, they would typically rally the troops. Starting with large meetings throughout the company with all eyes on the savior preaching their visions in a flood of I Have's, Me's and Mine's. The next step was to implement their vision, company wide. Usually, an army of middle managers were enlisted to spew out the savior's vision to the masses. After all, the savior was too busy and important to be tasked with the menial work of plan execution.

The leaders that truly brought change and growth always took a radical approach. They listened first. Void of the monotonous self-promotion and clichés, their first task was to understand.

The servant's quest typically began with small meetings. Lots of them. Gone were the mass indoctrinations with non-stop demands and platitudes. In their place were small group conversations that rarely revolved around the

> Remember the prisoners, as though in prison with them, and those who are ill-treated, since you yourselves also are in the body.
>
> Hebrews 13:3

leader. Typically, servants start with a simple question like, *"What can we do to help you do your job better?"*

Like peeling the skin off an onion, the servant would work to understand each person and their perception of the company. Deep in conversation, the small group, usually a team from the same department, would detail problems. Typically, the person who voiced a concern, would follow up with a recommended resolution rooted in "first-hand" experience. It didn't seem to matter the person's status or pay grade; they were always encouraged to participate in the conversation and become an integral part of the plan.

This approach always impressed me in its effectiveness. Not just in the meeting, but more importantly, as the strategy was rolled out. Every participant took ownership in the plan. They took it personally; becoming evangelists embedded in their departments; full of passion and resolve to ensure the success of "their" strategy.

You might be thinking the answer is simple. Just find Servants and put them in charge. In my experience, it always seemed that the "Saviors" dramatically outnumbered the "Servants," leading me to wonder… how could that be? Why is it that saviors always rise to the top of the ladder?

> "THE ONLY TIME YOU LOOK IN YOUR NEIGHBOR'S BOWL IS TO MAKE SURE THAT THEY HAVE ENOUGH. YOU DON'T LOOK IN YOUR NEIGHBOR'S BOWL TO SEE IF YOU HAVE AS MUCH AS THEM."
>
> Louis C.K.

The Canine Connection

While there are a lot of saviors in our lives, at work, in our churches, and even in our families, it is vital to know it is not their selfishness that gives them power. Instead, their power comes from us. In a sense, we appoint them to the role of savior, usually with welcome arms.

Most likely, this is not a conscious decision by us; it is more a gift of empowerment over our lives. If you are familiar with dogs, wolves and the canine species, you would recognize this trait as "Alpha" dogs. While most of the initial actions taken by a potential "Alpha" are aggressive and dominating; it is the "pack" that concedes and relinquishes power. After all, if the whole pack decided to take on the Alpha, aggression and dominating tactics wouldn't be enough to stop the entire pack. Appointing the aggressive, self-centered dog to lead the pack as their defender, their "Savior" is simply an act of protection for the group. Like our canine friends, we will tolerate a lot in trade for protection and security.

We always know who the Alpha is, even in a crowded room. They stand out; full of flash, excitement, enthusiasm, and sadly, themselves. You can't miss them; they just couldn't tolerate that. How is it that ego seems so rampant in our leaders? Leaders fixated on themselves. Again, it's not their fault.

It is our human passion and desire to be successful that drive us to be revered in the eyes of others. Deep inside, most of us want to be the Alpha. If not the recognition, we certainly covet the perks and the lifestyle. Not unlike those adolescent years in school full of cliques and condescension; we strive to be part of the "cool kids." Finding comfort in conformity, hoping we will be invited to sit at the cool kid's table, awash in its rebellious compliance.

> Help carry one another's burdens, and in this way you will obey the law of Christ.
>
> Galatians 6:2 GNT

Saviors and Alphas have been around since the first man walked the planet, albeit absent of the empathy associated with servants we know from scripture, like Christ Jesus and Mary Magdalene. Saviors are typically extreme narcissists that have convinced themselves that what they are doing is for the good of all. To them, it's just a side benefit that they gain wealth and power, even though the gain for them is typically at the core of their motivation.

112

Names like Napoleon, Hitler, and Castro come to mind. They were replete in their greed-driven power grabs, full of the promise of comfort and prosperity, while leaving chaos and destruction in their wake. These obvious tyrants masquerading as saviors caused untold devastation. However, the more subtle saviors bring about real destruction. Cults, money scams, and corporate greed are good examples of the subtle domination of saviors disguised as protection and kindness. My favorite tale of a destructive savior comes from Britain in the middle ages.

> ## "IF WE CAN SHARE OUR STORY WITH SOMEONE WHO RESPONDS WITH EMPATHY AND UNDERSTANDING, SHAME CAN'T SURVIVE."
>
> Brené Brown, Daring Greatly

The Lancelot Syndrome

The story of King Arthur and his Knights of the Round Table are legendary. For centuries, scholars have pored over the text of the story detailing the correlation with the Bible. Granted, there are several parallels in the story. However, most will tell you that Arthur was a Christ-like character, making him the obvious savior. For me, Arthur, like Christ, was more the servant king. My experience with so many corporate saviors always led me to think more of Sir Lancelot as the one who was always riding in on his White Horse to save the day. Literally.

In my assessment, Lancelot was not the Christ-inspired character in the story. In contrast, it is my belief he was more like Satan than Christ. While Lancelot did some good stuff; did he do anything that didn't benefit himself? In the end, it was his selfish desires that destroyed the Kingdom. That's what our Alpha Saviors do. Their narcissism and personal rewards drive their every step, leaving chaos and destruction everywhere they "save."

You might be thinking, *"Wait a minute, Lancelot did some great things."* He did. He also destroyed Camelot with his vain pursuits. What might have happened had Lancelot stayed focused on helping others and the Kingdom? Instead of fighting everyone's battles for them, what if Lancelot worked to understand Camelot's weaknesses, rather than jumping on his white horse to save the day? What if Lancelot shared his knowledge and training? What if he focused on making the other knights better warriors?

As you go through life, be watchful of saviors in your personal life or at work. For me, they have always been easy to identify. While they might not have Lancelot's shiny armor and white horse, you can't miss their constant use of the Savior's Credo; **"I Have, Me and Mine."**

> Love one another warmly as Christians and be eager to show respect for one another.
>
> **Romans 12:10 GNT**

Following Christ's command to love one another, even those who might hurt us, always led me to work with most of the saviors in my life. Doing whatever possible, guiding them to work to understand before they work to be understood. Even Saviors can be Servants when they learn empathy.

EMPATHY

"No one cares how much
you know, until they
know how much you care"

Theodore Roosevelt

LOVE PEOPLE with COMPASSION!

LOVE IN ACTION

LOVE GOD, LOVE PEOPLE

So many of us have grown accustomed to being saved. For me, the help of others is usually viewed as a blessing. When people have come into my life offering to save me from my current peril, my arms were typically wide open, and my heart was filled with gratitude. After all, don't we all love it when others help? Do you know some dependable helpers that always seemed to be there, and willing to help? Like Lancelot, riding in to "save the day."

Through the years, our life has been filled with so many wonderful people offering help without thought for themselves, or rewards. We learned that they were few and far between. In a lot of cases it seemed my saviors always had a reason to help. A benefit for them as well as me. What could be wrong with that? Wasn't it a "win-win" scenario? It seemed okay by me that they reaped rewards for themselves when helping me.

> Be of the same mind toward one another; do not be haughty in mind, but associate with the lowly. Do not Be wise in your own estimation.
>
> Romans 12:16

Over time, it appeared those same people would always be around, wanting to jump in and save me from the latest catastrophe as long as they got what they needed. It made me wonder; who were they helping, me or them? Thankfully, God led me to recognize some key differences between the saviors and servants in my life.

EMPATHY

At the center of most of the conversations with the saviors in my life were those words: *I, Me, and Mine.* Do you know people who start their loving advice with comments like, "What I would do," ... or, "If it were me ..."? While they sound caring, those words can point to thoughts that are more focused on them than you. In contrast, the servants will usually start with questions like "What do you need?"; "What would help you?" While they might seem like subtle differences, pinpointing whether someone's focus is on you or them says a lot about their motivation to help.

> "WHEN YOU SHOW DEEP
> EMPATHY TOWARD OTHERS,
> THEIR DEFENSIVE ENERGY GOES
> DOWN, AND POSITIVE ENERGY
> REPLACES IT. THAT'S WHEN
> YOU CAN GET MORE CREATIVE
> IN SOLVING PROBLEMS."
>
> Stephen Covey

So, what do you do? When there is something in it for them, are we to deny others trying to help? No. For me, following Stephen Covey's advice to "seek to understand" applies to saviors and servants as well. Isn't it as simple as understanding why someone wants to help?

So often we hear how clear communication leads to successful relationships. An honest relationship is built on trust with clarity and can only be achieved through transparent interaction with each other.

Love PEOPLE with COMPASSION!

When we know why someone is doing something to help, there are no surprise endings. Knowing someone's motivation to help, and seeing it come to fruition, always brings joy. On the other hand, when surprised by someone's reward for helping me, it always makes me wonder if it was all just a scam to benefit them.

Instead of burying our heads in the sands of ignorance, it is always best to have our eyes wide open through our awareness of the motivation of others. Ultimately, isn't it our unwillingness to understand that can lead to friction in relationships, destroying trust?

LOVE PEOPLE with COMPASSION BY:

"Seeking to be a Servant First!"

God is always fair. He will remember how you helped his people in the past and how you are still helping them. You belong to God, and he won't forget the love you have shown his people.
Hebrews 6:10 CEV

UNDERSTANDING

PEACE BE STILL

CHAPTER 8

"AND THE PEACE OF
GOD, WHICH SURPASSES
ALL UNDERSTANDING,
WILL GUARD YOUR
HEARTS AND MINDS IN
CHRIST JESUS."

PHILIPPIANS 4:7 NAS

Love IS the Answer!

From my earliest memory, my dream was to be an artist. Not Monet, Picasso, or Rembrandt. My artistic heroes were Bob Kane (Batman), Gil Kane (Green Lantern), and Norman Mingo (Mad Magazine). Always thinking my life would be spent drawing comic book characters led me away from schoolwork.

After all, who needs *"reading, 'riting & 'rithmatic"* to draw comic books?

120

UNDERSTANDING

My dream probably started around the age of six and grew stronger as the years passed. At eleven, starting sixth grade, my dream found a mentor, Mrs. Erikson. As my very first art teacher, she was full of love and enthusiasm. Her shiny blue eyes would light up with anyone's artistic accomplishment.

A small, thin woman in her late forties, Mrs. Erikson's face was always aglow and smiling like a child on Christmas morning. Her love and passion were contagious. She taught me so many things about art and about life. It was Mrs. Erikson who taught me to see beauty in everything. Teaching us all to appreciate the beauty of our world; from the design of a butterfly wing to the colors in a rainbow, she would always say, *"There's beauty in the details! No matter how big or small."*

> "DON'T PUT LIMITS ON YOURSELF. NOT EVERY DREAM WILL COME TRUE, AND NOT EVERY DREAM IS FROM GOD.
>
> BUT WHEN YOUR DREAMS CONNECT WITH GOD'S PLANS, YOU'LL FIND OPEN DOORS THAT YOU NEVER THOUGHT YOU'D SEE."
>
> Max Lucado

Mrs. Erikson's loving kindness inspired my drive to be an artist. She never "pigeonholed" her students into artistic boxes. (This one a painter, that one a sculptor, and such.) She encouraged us to create what was in our hearts. For me, it was my cartooning and my character, "Pete Neat."

Probably a juvenile knockoff of Bob Kane's "Cool McCool," Pete was a private detective. A little *Dick Tracy* meets *Spy vs. Spy* (Mad Magazine) with a lot of *Elvis*. That was Pete Neat. Always supportive of my drawing, Mrs. Erikson would continually challenge me to look at different ways to express my art. Pottery, wood sculpture, painting and even papier mâché. It was Mrs. Erikson who taught me to always follow my dreams.

Beginning junior high school in the throes of Beatlemania, my focus quickly shifted to becoming the next Paul McCartney, pushing art on the back burner. At the end of seventh grade, along with two friends, we started a band cleverly named, "It's All in Your Mind." While we sounded horrible, we looked great. For me, it was Beatle hair, knee-high moccasins and my prize possession, a Höfner bass guitar, just like Paul's. Later that year, the three of us parted ways as friends, ending our dreams of becoming the next pop sensation.

My parents divorced that year, resulting in my move to Dallas, Texas, in the summer with my dad. My dad traveled all over the country with work, so my days and nights were pretty lonesome. In Texas, football is a religion. Not playing football seemed to put me on the outside looking in, always feeling like the weird kid with a funny Iowa accent.

A friend loves at all times, And a brother is born for adversity.

Proverbs 17:17

It was that isolated time in Texas when "Pete Neat" came back to life. God used Pete to introduce me to what would later be called my "happy place," a place of escape inside my art where my cares would disappear like "smoke in the wind." Still, the loneliness consumed all of me with a deep longing for home. Within a couple of months, it was back to Iowa.

Going back to my old junior high school brought mixed emotions. While it was great to be on familiar turf, starting a couple of months into the new school year felt strange and awkward. Kids that were once friends now treated me like a stranger.

The one bright light that year was Mr. Reese, my art teacher. A rough and tough macho kinda guy, he was the furthest thing from what you would expect an eighth-grade art teacher to look or act like. It was Mr. Reese who re-ignited my dream to be an artist. He was encouraging and full of energy. Setting aside Pete and my dream of comic books, Mr. Reese expanded my imagination beyond illustration. Teaching basic principles, he set my artistic approach for the rest of my life. Primarily, he helped me to understand that while it was my art, and it is critical to "own" your art, it is also important to

"ANY FOOL CAN KNOW. THE POINT IS TO UNDERSTAND."

Albert Einstein

consider my audience. Asking myself, *"What will they see?"* then working to make my art appreciated by others, instead of only me. This was the beginning of my "walk a mile in their shoes" philosophy.

The summer between eighth and ninth grade found me cruising around town on my bike looking for friends and anything to stop the boredom. One hot, humid July morning at a local swimming pool, there were a bunch of people hanging around a convertible, laughing and joking with each other. At the center of the foolishness, was a nineteen-year-old guy who was playing loud music while teasing everyone in sight. We quickly became friends and he would set me on a path that changed my life. There are too many stories to cover in this book, but it was that summer and his friendship that led me out my loneliness and propelled me into maturity.

Hanging out with a group of older friends, along with the freedom from responsibility as a child of an alcoholic, single mother, added years of maturity. As summer came to a close, the thirteen-year-old boy that wore his new-found freedom as a badge of honor felt like he was returning to school with the heart and head of an eighteen-year-old man.

Cynical of most of my teachers and anyone in authority, my disdain for school was beginning to take hold. One of my first classes in ninth grade was art with Mrs. Astrid, a frail, older lady known for her grumpy demeanor and strict discipline. Fighting back sour memories of her art class in seventh grade and walking into the room, trying to not be noticed while looking for an empty desk, Mrs. Astrid saw me and shouted out with a huge smile, *"Mark, I'm so glad you're here!"* Puzzled, watching her walk quickly back to my desk made me wonder if this could be the same woman. Gone was the scowl of condemnation; her face was glowing with bright blue eyes of her own. Standing in front of me she gleefully said, *"Mr. Reese has told me so much about you, and what a talent you are. We're going to have a great time together!"* This was the beginning of one of my favorite times in school, and the once grumpy Mrs. Astrid became my favorite art teacher of all time.

> *"If a kingdom is divided against itself, that kingdom cannot stand. "If a house is divided against itself, that house will not be able to stand.*
>
> Mark 3:24-25

The year before my eighth grade, in an attempt to desegregate public schools, our city had begun busing African American students into our school. While several students hated it and treated the kids on the bus horribly, for me, they were a welcome addition.

UNDERSTANDING

It was my good fortune to grow up across the street from a wonderful African American family full of love and joy. Their youngest daughter was a great friend in my early years, and our friendship taught me that all people are people; nothing more and nothing less. Watching my dad argue with our neighbors about the family's right to live in the neighborhood and seeing him stand up for the rights of others always made me proud.

In the late sixties, our country was more torn apart over race than any other time in our history. The year 1968 saw the assassination of Dr. Martin Luther King and Bobby Kennedy. Three short years after the bloody riots in the Los Angeles suburb of Watts, race tensions were intense with Dr. King's death and the injustice of young African American boys drafted to fight the war in Vietnam.

> "EVERYTHING THAT IRRITATES
> US ABOUT OTHERS CAN LEAD
> US TO AN UNDERSTANDING
> OF OURSELVES"
>
> Carl Jung

Most would think that the sleepy Iowa town of Des Moines would be immune from the hatred and division. Maybe fifty years earlier, but with a TV in every house, the riots, the war, and all the hatred were nightly events around the dinner table. Or, more accurately, the TV tray.

The division and hatred we watched every night was carried into school. Both sides, Blacks and Whites, would have nothing to do with each other. Not really the end to segregation that had been expected. For me, busing kids always seemed to be more about politics than trying to bring folks together.

In ninth grade, one night playing basketball after school, God introduced me to my best friend, Tony: A tall, lanky African American who was the embodiment of what African American boys looked like in the late sixties: T-shirt, jeans and an Afro that would have made Michael Jackson jealous. We hit it off immediately. Most nights after basketball, we would hang around talking about school, sports, and everything that was going on in the world. We both agreed it was pretty silly for people to treat each other with such hate. After a particularly bad day, we talked about how we were both being bullied; me by African American kids, Tony by the White kids, which led us to make a pact. Tony would stand up for me with his friends while my friends would answer to me when they picked on Tony. We found comfort and security in our trusting friendship.

> "Do not judge, and you will not be judged; and do not condemn, and you will not be condemned; pardon, and you will be pardoned.
>
> Luke 6:37

One night after basketball, toward the end of the school year, we were talking about what's next and our thoughts of going to high school. Tony said his uncle had helped him to enroll in a "technical" high school so he could learn auto mechanics. Not giving it much thought, he heard my plan to follow in my sister and brother's footsteps by going to the high school in our neighborhood. He knew my dissatisfaction in going to a school with a reputation for football and keggers, instead of a school where my art would be appreciated and nurtured.

The next day at lunch, Tony came running up to me with a big smile. *"You'll never believe this!"* Trying to catch his breath, he continued, *"I was talking with my uncle last night and he told me there's a great art program at the technical high school."*

He went on to say, *"They offer commercial art as a 'core' curriculum."* Tony explained, *"You take all the English, math and history classes in the morning, then you spend all afternoon in your core program, art."* We were both excited about the idea of continuing our friendship. Eating lunch was a blur as we talked about going to high school on the "buddy plan," all the way to graduation. Before long, it was summer, and we would say goodbye until high school.

> ## "DARKNESS CANNOT DRIVE OUT DARKNESS; ONLY LIGHT CAN DO THAT. HATE CANNOT DRIVE OUT HATE; ONLY LOVE CAN DO THAT."
>
> DR. MARTIN LUTHER KING, JR.

Feeding Frenzy

Have you ever noticed how people change when they are part of a group? Like in the animal and insect world, groups seem to take on a personality of their own. For example, a docile honeybee by itself won't bother you. Using its stinger only for protection, the lone bee goes about its business of pollination; can you think of a more serene existence? Or, how about the solitary locust? Jumping from one spot to the next in complete bliss.

Why is it when they are in swarms and are threatened, they turn into a ferocious and fearsome fury? A frenzy. You might be thinking it's all about protection and in a way, it is.

The definition of frenzy is "a temporary madness" or "a violent mental or emotional agitation." Synonyms of frenzy include deliriousness, fury, hysteria, rage, and rampage.

Does that surprise you? How could a passive locust go on a hysterical rampage?

What takes the docile bee and locust and transforms them into a frenzied group? Experts will tell you it is all about survival: "fight or flight;" the cortisol effect. Whether it's a herd of gazelles fleeing in a frenzy while running off a cliff, or the lions chasing them in a feeding frenzy, isn't that just about survival? The gazelle at the bottom of the cliff would probably disagree.

In a failed sequel to the blockbuster film, *The Exorcist*, Hollywood reunited some of the original cast, along with Academy Award winner Richard Burton, in hopes of recreating the box office success of the original movie with a sequel. Even with Richard Burton, *Exorcist II* is considered one of the worst films ever made. If you have

> What the gnawing locust has left, the swarming locust has eaten; And what the swarming locust has left, the creeping locust has eaten; And what the creeping locust has left, the stripping locust has eaten.
>
> Joel 1:4

seen the movie, you know why. Dark and drawn out with a minimal plot, it was Burton, one of my favorite actors, that attracted me to see the movie, in an empty theater.

The premise of the movie was based on something called, "Touching of the Wings," referencing the locusts of the African plains. The movie proposed that it was the closeness of the individual locusts that created the frenzy. When their wings touch, an evil force takes over the swarm. When an individual locust feels trapped among the others, for its survival it must eat as much as it can.

UNDERSTANDING

When all the individual locusts feel trapped, they all eat as much as possible. Swarming, the once docile insects become a voracious, unstoppable and unrelenting force.

While most of the movie is now forgotten, the concept of the touching wings has never left me. Don't we see it all the time? Whether it's in the animal world or in the animal of man. When restrained and endangered with others, doesn't the group react in ways an individual would never do? Is it all in the name of survival? Or, as the movie suggested, is it an evil force formed by the touching of the wings?

It is our fear that drives us to a group for protection. When fear grips the heart of our group, it is the collective fear that embraces evil as an answer.

> "THERE IS POWER IN
> UNDERSTANDING THE
> JOURNEY OF OTHERS TO
> HELP CREATE YOUR OWN..."
> Kobe Bryant

In my experience, isolated individuals are not consumed by the hatred and rage found in their groups. What would the German soldiers of WW II say about how they would treat others? Wouldn't most deny any hatred? Sadly, it is when individuals become part of a group, shrouded in fear, they become frenzied and hateful. They are set off by a few evil individuals who guide them to commit unthinkable atrocities. Running off the cliff of hate and brutality like a herd of gazelles fleeing in a frenzy of fear.

You might be thinking... what do locusts, bees, and frenzies have to do with Tony and me? Well, starting high school that year introduced me to the evil frenzy and hatred of racism.

The summer before high school was filled with "keggers" or parties almost every night. My transformation into adulthood continued with experiences that most people wouldn't go through until college. When it was time to go back to school, Tony was a distant memory, making me wonder if a technical school was the right thing. The high school with the party reputation was beginning to look like it might be fun.

Sitting in the auditorium of the vocational school that first day for freshman orientation while trying to find Tony is when it hit me, this school was very different than my junior high school. It was easy to find Tony back at our old school. He always stood out as an African American student in a huge crowd of White kids. Here, the auditorium was filled with boys who looked like Tony. Now, it was me who was in the minority. Thinking to myself, with all the hate in the world, this could be a scary place without Tony in my corner.

Let all bitterness and wrath and anger and clamor and slander be put away from you, along with all malice.

Ephesians 4:31

Like before, there was no interaction between the African American students and the White kids. Not being able to spot him, my mind wandered to the unthinkable, what if Tony had changed his mind? Scanning every face in the auditorium became a desperate act, until the sound of that unmistakable laugh bellowed out loud; there he was! Tony finally looked right at me and my waving arms. But there was no smile, no wave; he quickly turned away as if he was trying to not look back. After the assembly, Tony was nowhere to be found. Then it was off to my first class in high school.

Sitting by myself in the cafeteria that first day at lunch was unnerving. It didn't feel very welcoming at all. Then, there was Tony, joking around with a bunch of his friends. And me, walking up to say *Hi!* with a big smile; he almost acted like he didn't know me. Whispering, he said, *"Hey Mark, how's it going?"* His behavior was puzzling, gone was my happy and jovial friend; now he seemed almost embarrassed to know me. A huge guy sitting at his table shouted, *"Tony, whatcha doing with that honky?"* With that, Tony in a still and very quiet voice said, *"I'll catch up with you later, Mark,"* and sat back down with his friends.

It wasn't until a few days later that it became clear what was going on. The same guy that yelled at Tony during lunch walked up to me between classes, pushing me into the lockers, getting up in my face. Then he grunted, *"Tony don't need no friends like you. All you'll do is bring pain down on him. Stay away from him or else!"* Shortly after my encounter with

> ## "PEACE CANNOT BE ACHIEVED THROUGH VIOLENCE, IT CAN ONLY BE ATTAINED THROUGH UNDERSTANDING."
>
> Ralph Waldo Emerson

the locker, Tony walked by. He looked horrible. Puffy eyes, bruises, and a swollen lip. Glancing at me he just shook his head and walked past.

That was the last time we saw each other. Sadly, it wasn't my last experience with the lockers. From that day forward, every walk through the halls on the way to class was like going through a gauntlet of punches, trips, and locker smashes. Telling the teachers or administrators about it did no good; their only suggestion was to avoid the people who were picking on me. How do you avoid walking through hallways to get to class?

When talking with other students about the beatings, they all said they had no difficulties, leading me to think it was all about my friendship with Tony. Unfortunately, it seemed that the worst thing a White kid could do was be friends with an African American. Well, it only took a few months to ask for a transfer back to my original high school. It was either that or face the gauntlet every hour of every school day.

Someone once asked me if there was forgiveness in my heart for how Tony treated me. It might surprise you to know my feelings for Tony were always loving and have never changed. If anything, my heart was full of empathy. For me, it was as simple as transferring schools to get back to my life. With Tony, he needed to go home at night and get along with his family and friends or face an unending gauntlet of his own. It broke my heart to know the bigotry that Tony, his family, and friends faced daily would never end until, as Dr. King taught, we learn to *"judge each other by the content of our character, and not the color of our skin."*

> *Pride goes before destruction, a haughty spirit before a fall.*
> **Proverbs 16:18 NIV**

While some would point to my short time at the tech school as a horrendous experience, for me, it was a pivotal life lesson. One that is more a blessing than a curse. That short time as a minority taught me to always work to understand the plight of others. Facing the hate and bitterness that comes with racial discrimination opened my eyes to all that was going on in our country. The nightly news now made sense.

Through navigating the gauntlet multiple times a day, there was only one thought on my mind: Freedom. To live my life free of all of the hatred and threats of violence. My fears consumed me every moment of every day. Thinking that the people marching for equality on TV were living their entire lives embroiled in that kind of fear and hatred gave me an understanding that can only come through experience.

God used this knowledge to show me the destruction caused by bigotry. As a personal understanding, those few short months revealed the vicious outcomes born through intolerance. Today, we see bigotry everywhere. Not just between races. We see it between factions and divisions in our society. Left vs. right, blue collar vs. white collar, men vs. women, young vs. old, and so many more. We seem to find our bully nature in groups, where it is generated by group hatred.

> "TRY TO UNDERSTAND MEN.
> IF YOU UNDERSTAND EACH
> OTHER YOU WILL BE KIND
> TO EACH OTHER.
>
> KNOWING A MAN WELL
> NEVER LEADS TO HATE
> AND ALMOST ALWAYS
> LEADS TO LOVE."
>
> John Steinbeck

Sadly, it just takes a few evil instigators to stir up a frenzy of hatred in people gathered together with a common mindset. There is no doubt that each one of the guys hitting me between classes was just like Tony. Probably great guys with good hearts. Every day in those hallways, it was like a feeding frenzy. It just took one guy to start, and before long, every guy there was getting their licks in, convinced they were doing the right thing.

One of the most popular scriptures in the Bible is Galatians 5:22-23, which describes the Fruit of the Spirit. The Fruit of the Spirit is Love and the other virtues found in these verses are "acts" of love: kindness, joy, peace, goodness, faithfulness, self-control, gentleness, and patience; all define different virtues of Love.

On the other hand, one of the least known scriptures seems to be the three verses right before, Galatians 5:19-21. It is this scripture that the Apostle Paul describes the "acts" of the flesh. Paul explains that those who practice such obvious things as greed, lust, and immorality will not inherit the kingdom of God. Severe sins indeed. It might surprise you that divisiveness and factionalism are on the same list, as well as idolatry, rage, and jealousy. All factors of hate found in groups. So, when we break into groups or factions, separating the body of Christ through divisiveness

> Treat others just as you want to be treated.
>
> Luke 6:31 CEV

and bigotry, we are deep in sin. God wants us to glorify Him as individuals, not groups. He cares about what is in our heart, not what group we belong to.

In Christ we are called to soar like eagles. However, when we swarm with others in a group, we find our wings touching, leading us to succumb to the evil created by group thinking and not our own. Group fear ignites into a frenzy of irrational and hateful actions. Darkness will seize a group placing importance of the group itself over individuals, and over God. This is a form of idolatry, as is anything we position between ourselves and God.

There is no doubt that Tony cared about me. Still, when faced with the powerful influence of the group, he gave in to the pressure. While he never participated in my hourly gauntlets, by turning away and not standing up for what he believed and knew was right, he condoned each and every punch, trip, and push.

UNDERSTANDING

My dad taught me so many lessons. One of my favorites was, "No action is an action." He would always say that it is our inaction that creates the unwanted circumstances of our lives. Don't we usually know the right thing to do? Often in my life it was the reasoning and justification of my bad actions that led me down some dark roads, all the while knowing in my heart the right thing to do. It was my rationale of those bad decisions that created an untold number of "coulda, woulda, shoulda's throughout my life.

It is my belief that most bigotry is fueled by a few evil people. It is our inability or unwillingness to stand up to the hatred; to be the eagles God wants us to be, that we allow the evil of bigotry to turn into a frenzy of hate.

> "NOTHING IN LIFE IS TO BE FEARED, IT IS ONLY TO BE UNDERSTOOD. NOW IS THE TIME TO UNDERSTAND MORE, SO THAT WE MAY FEAR LESS."
>
> Maria Skłodowska-Curie

My experience in those hallways of hate could have taken me down a road of vitriol and loathing. Thus, blaming an entire race of people for all the pain and suffering caused by a few in a frenzy of hate. Thankfully, God opened my eyes to understand hatred and bigotry from their perspective. A lesson that will never be forgotten.

LOVE IN ACTION
SEEK FIRST TO UNDERSTAND!

Doesn't it feel good to be accepted? To be one of the "in crowd" or the "cool kids"? While most of my life was spent on the outside looking in, there were times when others were envious of my life and my friends. During ninth grade, my nineteen-year-old friend would pick me up from junior high school in his convertible. The look of envy in the eyes of the kids in my school made me feel superior as they watched me and a car full of older kids take off for another night of partying. As the year went on, my classmates' envy turned into jealousy, leading most everyone in school to shun me. Without my friendship with Tony, ninth grade would have been a very lonely place. An arrogant spirit is usually the first sign of an impending fall.

It is the fear of isolation and a need to feel accepted that drives our craving to be part of a group. Groups provide more than camaraderie. They bring members protection and encouragement, all the while making us proud to be part of something bigger than ourselves. It is the pride of the group and our fear of rejection that leads us to stand up for the group, even when we disagree with the direction it may be going. The fear of isolation or being disliked is a powerful force; a force that is hard to overcome.

> Let no one look down on your youthfulness, but rather in speech, conduct, love, faith and purity, show yourself an example of those who believe.
>
> 1 Timothy 4:12

UNDERSTANDING

So many times, it was my fear of being pushed out of a group for standing up for my beliefs that led to my silence. Or worse, participation in group thinking and hatred leading me to an undesirable action. All the while, working to protect the group from others while worrying about the group's perception of me.

After my experiences during those first few months of high school, it became clear to me that there are two separate forces of relationships at work in our lives. Personal, individual relationships and those that come with a group of like-minded people. Christ taught us to "Love One Another" as individuals, not as a group.

Many times, we put the desires of the group above what we know to be the right thing to do as an individual. In a sense, we place our group on a pedestal; reveling in the power that comes in numbers. In my experience, this is a form of idol worship. Often my desire to please the group would lead me away from doing the right thing, driving me away from God.

> "PEACE CANNOT BE KEPT
> BY FORCE; IT CAN
> ONLY BE ACHIEVED
> BY UNDERSTANDING."
>
> Albert Einstein

When confronted with that gut-wrenching decision to do "the right thing" or the wrong, more expedient thing, when standing my ground and not giving in to the group, some of the best things in my life happened. We've all been there. Angel whispering in one ear, devil in the other. Don't you truly always know the right thing to do? It seemed all my anxiety came from me justifying doing what was wrong (the bad decision), while every "good decision" washed me with calm and peace.

Developing the habit of praying every time these situations would arise made it easier to stand up to a group mindset. "If God is for us, who can be against us?" Like exercise, when you develop the habit of doing the right thing, you get stronger and the task becomes easier. The content of our character is built over time, like building muscles through exercise with unrelenting discipline and perseverance.

LOVE PEOPLE with COMPASSION BY:

"Looking at Life through Their Eyes!"

"I HAVE A DREAM THAT MY FOUR LITTLE CHILDREN WILL ONE DAY LIVE IN A NATION WHERE THEY WILL NOT BE JUDGED BY THE COLOR OF THEIR SKIN,

BUT BY THE CONTENT OF THEIR CHARACTER."

Dr. Martin Luther King, Jr.

TRUST

A REASON TO BELIEVE

CHAPTER 9

"LOVE EACH OTHER
AS BROTHERS AND
SISTERS AND HONOR
OTHERS MORE THAN
YOU DO YOURSELF."
ROMANS 12:10 CEV

The Rock of Relationships

What would you say is the most important trait of the people in your life? How would you describe those closest to you? Does loving, kind and generous come to mind? Is that enough? What about integrity and trust? If you are like most of us, trust is at the top of the list for those true, deep relationships.

Without trust, is there really a relationship?

TRUST

How would you describe Trust? Is there a word you can you think of to replace it with? How about confidence? Faith or hope? Would caring or reliability explain how we trust each other? Trust is one of those words that stands alone. Like describing a color or a beautiful sunrise, words alone cannot explain what trust is. Isn't trust something we just know or feel; our "gut" feeling? Is that gnawing in our gut really just about trust? Explaining words like trust is like trying to describe something green. While there is a myriad of variations, green is green, but we can't explain it without a comparison to another color or something green.

The words that seem to fit trust for me revolve around relationship and love. Not the friendship kinda' love, but the unconditional love that a parent has for a child. More than just

> "THE WAY TO MAKE PEOPLE
> TRUST-WORTHY IS TO
> TRUST THEM."
>
> Ernest Hemingway

a friendship or acquaintance, but the deep, best-friend kind of a relationship we reserve for those special few. Hopefully, we all have those friends we would trust with our lives, or the lives of our families. That's the kind of relationship scripture tells us Jesus wants to have with us.

Aren't all great relationships built on trust? Trust cannot happen without a relationship, and relationships only exist through empathy, love and compassion for one another. Taking our focus off ourselves and concentrating on others, we find their trust. We are all vulnerable at times; helping others when they are vulnerable builds trust in one another. Without trust, there is only friendship or acquaintance.

LOVE PEOPLE with COMPASSION!

When we first meet someone, do we automatically find trust? It takes time and devotion to build history and understanding with another person. While most of us have some trust when we meet someone new; typically, it is not that "Lay Down My Life for You!" kind of trust. Most of us have faith that others will do "the right thing." It is only when we see our new acquaintance earn our trust over time, will our relationship grow strong. Trust is not about one big event; instead, we develop trust in small actions added to one another over time.

In my early twenties, with the prospect of a growing family and little mouths to feed, we made the decision to change jobs. This required leaving my beloved music industry to become a representative for a regional home appliance distributor. It was a dramatic change; walking away from an industry that was second nature to me, to a job calling on refrigerator and TV dealers in southern Iowa and Illinois. After my first year, the company made a change in territory management and added the "river cities" in southern Iowa and Illinois to my territory.

> *Be devoted to one another in love. Honor one another above yourselves.*
> **Romans 12:10 NIV**

Change never caused anxiety for me, the new business would be a welcomed and exciting addition. No longer would my territory consist of the mostly smaller "Mom & Pop" dealers in towns like Ottumwa, Oskaloosa, and Grinnell. Finally, there were sprawling metro areas like Burlington, Keokuk, and Muscatine. Probably not considered cities by most, but for this Iowa boy, these sprawling towns were almost as exciting as my hometown, Des Moines.

With the bigger cities, came BIG dealers! Well that's what everyone told me. The part they left out was BIG dealers carry "tier one" brands like Zenith, RCA, Maytag and Amana. While my products, Quasar, Panasonic, and Gibson were great, they were "tier two." It was almost an insult for a tier two sales rep to call on a tier one dealer. Added to my frustration was finding out that the owners of those BIG dealerships were all exceptionally busy. Keeping up with their hordes of customers made them hard to pin down. That's who Bob was, a BIG, busy, Tier One Dealer.

> ## "HAVE ENOUGH COURAGE TO TRUST LOVE ONE MORE TIME AND ALWAYS ONE MORE TIME"
>
> Maya Angelou

Owner of a huge appliance and furniture store in one of the bigger river cities, Bob was a third-generation proprietor of an entrenched merchant family. His store was so big, it even had an elevator, something almost unheard of in any store in his town, or most others in Iowa.

Bob's family started the business decades earlier with an extreme focus on serving customer needs as a "Pay as You Go" sales company. Everything in the store could be bought with weekly payments; no credit required. Truly, trusting strangers was their unique value-add in the small community. *"A happy customer always shops here first!"* Bob would constantly proclaim with a huge smile. It always impressed me that Bob's dealership was such a benefactor for the area. If your refrigerator broke, you could get the latest, greatest model with no money down and weekly payments.

Meeting with the sales rep who had the territory before me, we talked about all the dealers and all the towns. When we got to Bob, the rep made it clear it would be a waste of time

143

and energy to even call on Bob once. *"That guy's a jerk! No time for anyone, he takes pleasure in belittling anyone he talks to."* The rep continued, *"Besides, he doesn't need anything we sell, and you'll NEVER sell him anything!"* The rep might as well have just smacked me with a glove and challenged me to a duel at sunrise. The game was now afoot!

Planning my next week's travel, visiting Bob was at the top of the list. After arriving in town, and checking into my hotel the night before, it was time to cruise by Bob's store and get the "lay of the land" before my cold call the next day.

Driving by the closed store a little after 9 p.m., it looked dark and deserted. It was a classic small-town storefront on the main street, all brick, five stories high, and seemed as deep as it was tall. Looking in through the big picture window it was pitch black, except for a single light leaking onto the showroom floor from a room hidden from the street. Thinking that the store didn't seem so huge, it was back to the hotel to prepare for the big day.

> The king is the friend of all who are sincere and speak with kindness.
>
> **Proverbs 22:11 CEV**

Early morning breakfasts in Iowa were the best. Farm fresh everything: eggs, cheese, hash browns, pancakes and all the trimmings. Small town hotel restaurants were superb people observation venues. Watching regulars, travelers and visitors intermingling in a festival of morning rituals has always been a travel tradition when preparing my strategies for the day. This day had no strategy, just resolve. Resolve to knock this big bird off his perch. With a deep breath and a full stomach, it was off to meet the day!

Walking in the front door of the store, there was the loud clang of a bell hanging atop the frame. With that, everyone inside turned to give me the once over. No customers were in the store this early, just a gaggle of hungry salesmen by a coffee machine; coffee cup in one hand and cigarette in the other. Making my way through the long showroom with refrigerators lined up on both sides, most of the salesmen turned away, figuring that they weren't going to sell me anything. Except for that one eager guy who squeezed through the crowd. With a nervous smile and voice trembling, he said, *"Welcome, are you looking for a white refrigerator or is our new avocado more to your liking?"* Shaking hands, his nerves were made more obvious by the dampness of his palm. Asking, *"Is Bob in?"* my question seemed to increase his anxiety.

"TO BE TRUSTED IS A GREATER COMPLIMENT THAN BEING LOVED."

George MacDonald

Almost whispering, he quivered back, *"Mr. Hettinger is in his office, but he's not seeing anyone today."* With that, a short stout man appeared from the back office where the light was the night before. *"Tommy, who the hell is that?"* he grumbled, walking closer, sporting a Charlie Chaplin mustache, the charred remains of a cigarette hanging off his lower lip. Refilling a paper coffee cup, ashes falling in the cup he continued yelling... *"Tell that !#&#! to get the hell out of here! We don't need any of his crap!"* He swaggered back into his office, slamming the door.

"That's Bob," Tommy said with a humiliated smile. Spending the next hour talking to this young man, he told me that Bob was his uncle. It seemed Tommy's dad couldn't work with Bob and sent Tommy in to learn the family business.

It's still not clear to me why; walking out the door and hearing myself shout back, *"Thanks Tommy, see you in two weeks!"* made me think … "What was that?" Possibly some deep seated competitive ambition? Looking back today, it seems it was more like divine intervention. Spending the rest of the week in my territory, staring at the windshield of my car between stops, Tommy's puzzled face looking back at me always brought a smile.

Two weeks on the dot, that bell above the door clanged, as it did twice a month, for the next year. Always the same scene, a gaggle of salesmen, Tommy always emerging to greet me. As time went on, Tommy looked happy to see me. We would share stories about selling appliances. He would spice up our talks with tales of his uncle and his latest victims of vitriol. When, and where possible, it became my mission to teach Tommy whatever possible. Occasionally, Bob would pop out onto the floor shouting some disparagement at me like, *"How are sales?!"* or *"We sold thirty refrigerators yesterday, how about you!?"* Realizing that this one dealer was selling more in one day than my whole territory did in a week was frustrating. Bob knew my sales numbers and truly enjoyed the provocation, seeming to feed off the cheap shots and my unwillingness to push back. Bob would spend more time on the floor when it was my day to show up. He was like a peacock. strutting around and showing off this and that, while relentlessly teasing me. As we got to know each other, it was easy to see that he really knew his stuff. It wasn't just hot air he was blowing; Bob clearly knew the cold hard facts of the appliance world.

> A friend loves at all times, And a brother is born for adversity.
> Proverbs 17:17

One day walking in the door, with the clanging of the bell, my visit started out just like the rest, except for one thing. On this day, Bob was on the floor waiting for me. *"Come back to my office, I gotta ask you something."*

Bewildered and feeling like a peasant going into the King's court; or a pig going to slaughter, curious all the while about what prank Bob had up his sleeve. Walking into the dimly lit, smoky room, the first thing that caught my eye were the bookcases lining the walls. From floor to ceiling, each one was overstuffed with three ring binders crammed in every nook and cranny of those worn out shelves.

> "WHEN WE CAN TALK ABOUT
> OUR FEELINGS, THEY BECOME
> LESS OVERWHELMING,
> LESS UPSETTING,
> AND LESS SCARY.
>
> THE PEOPLE WE TRUST
> WITH THAT IMPORTANT TALK
> CAN HELP US KNOW THAT
> WE ARE NOT ALONE."
>
> Fred "Mr" Rogers

There he was, sitting behind his huge desk, strewn with newspapers full of his latest ads. Off to the side was a dirty, smelly, overflowing ashtray, stuffed with ugly cigarette butts that looked like they had been there for years. A green banker's lamp shed a bright light on Bob's most recent ad. Brushing away cigarette ash off his desk, he asked, *"What do you think of this week's ad?"* Full of doubt, my first thought was, what's the joke, where's the trap? After looking things over it seemed legit, it was a great ad.

Bob didn't know that as a kid, my dad taught me ad composition as part of my job helping with his business. Like Bob, my skills were strong. Pointing out a few flow issues with his layout seemed to impress him.

Well, from that day forward my visits at Bob's store always started in his office, we became close friends as he continued to seek my advice. It was my pleasure and honor to help. Those little steps built a strong, trusting relationship.

A year and half after hearing that bell clang the first time, sitting in his office, going over the newest ad, Bob reclined in his chair, looked me in the eye, and asked, *"What the hell do you do this for?"* He seemed genuinely confused. Shaking his head, he added, *"You come here like clockwork, helping with my ads. Why?"*

> The righteous is a guide to his neighbor, But the way of the wicked leads them astray.
> Proverbs 12:26

Now, you might think that question was expected, but it wasn't. Looking for words to say, my mouth just started moving, *"Well, it is important for me to know that you are aware of the kind of service and support you'll get when you're my dealer."* Pushing back the humiliation of my sappy comment and surprised to see Bob's eyes tear up, he barked, *"I think you're nuts! But I'm glad you started coming in."*

You've probably already guessed. Bob continued to be a great friend and a revered mentor. The following year, Bob became one of my biggest dealers and my favorite success story.

Like my relationship with Bob, trust was built one small step at a time. When we build our relationships on a rock of trust; the foundation will support us through every storm in life. The rock of our relationship was built on trust. It was only after forging that relationship, that Bob was able trust me. He knew that my focus was on him, his business, and most importantly, his customers. Bob had comfort knowing he could trust me with the business his family had entrusted to him.

The rock that Jesus taught us to stand on, to build our house on, is that rock of trust. We are not to build our house on our confidence, our faith, or our hope in Him or in each other. We are to build our relationships on trust. Trust in each other and trust in Him.

"FORGIVENESS MUST BE
IMMEDIATE, WHETHER OR
NOT A PERSON ASKS FOR IT.
TRUST MUST BE REBUILT OVER
TIME. TRUST REQUIRES
A TRACK RECORD."

Rick Warren, The Purpose Driven Life

LOVE In ACTION

GUARD YOUR HEART

Have you ever been in a situation that made you anxious? You couldn't place where the fear was coming from or what is was you should be concerned about? The knot in your stomach was growing and the butterflies were turning into a swarm of bees. What causes that? How do you know something is wrong? Would it surprise you to know it was biological and it is how you are made?

My first time walking through the streets of Manhattan by myself were horrific. It felt as if there was a cement block on each shoulder and my feet were sticking to the sidewalk like a muddy road after an Iowa thunderstorm. Petrified is the only word that may come

> A man of too many friends comes to ruin, But there is a friend who sticks closer than a brother.
>
> Proverbs 18:24

close to describing my feelings. Thinking it through, there was no logical reason to be afraid. It was still daytime and the streets were packed with people. Like my mom always told me, "There's safety in numbers." So why the fear?

It wasn't the big city. After all, we had lived in some big cities like Dallas, Washington D.C. and our current home, Philadelphia. What could be causing so much angst? It was my brain.

Growing up in Iowa, we would hear all the stories of crime and violence in New York City. Every night there was one crime story after another about how the New York Police

Department had foiled the plans of diabolical criminals or caught a serial killer. Movies like *Taxi Driver* and the latest gangster movies filled the theaters. All this knowledge of "The City" was packed deep inside my brain. Even though thoughts of crimes and criminals were not on my conscious mind, my sub-conscious was working overtime trying to keep me safe. All that pent-up knowledge was creating a "fight or flight" response in my internal warning system. My cortisol levels must have been off the charts, ready to flood my body with adrenaline at a moment's notice. Even though there was no logical reason to be afraid, my body had prepared itself for the worst. It took me years of traveling to New York City, even living there for a while before the feelings of fear subsided.

> ## "TRUST IS THE FRUIT OF A RELATIONSHIP IN WHICH YOU KNOW YOU ARE LOVED."
>
> Wm. Paul Young

Getting rid of my fear was not a conscious act. In fact, it was the opposite, it was my subconscious that eradicated the fear. Over time, working in Manhattan and getting to know New Yorkers as some of the most kind and loyal people on the planet whittled away at my deep seated fears. No longer was every New Yorker out to get me. Their kindness and "got your back" loyalty had replaced my fears with trust. A deep trust that told me if there was ever a problem, most anyone on the streets of New York would bend over backwards to help. To this day, it is that trust in who New Yorkers are that makes my heart jump when someone tells me they are from "the City."

So often it is what we are thinking, consciously or subconsciously, that gets in the way of what is truly happening around us. Scripture tells us to guard our hearts, for all things flow from our hearts. It doesn't say guard your brain. When we love God and love people, we stop listening to our brain and listen with our heart. Trusting in God is the fastest way to untie the knot in your stomach and get the butterflies to fly in formation.

LOVE PEOPLE with COMPASSION BY:

"Loving First, Giving First, Serving First,
and Trusting First!"

Iron sharpens iron,
So one man sharpens another.
Proverbs 27:17

152

LoveOthersLoudly

SECTION IV

"I APPEAL TO YOU, BROTHERS,
IN THE NAME OF OUR LORD JESUS CHRIST,
THAT ALL OF YOU AGREE TOGETHER,
SO THAT THERE MAY BE
NO DIVISIONS AMONG YOU
AND THAT YOU MAY BE UNITED
IN MIND AND CONVICTION."

1 Corinthians 1:10

LOVE PEOPLE
WITH
CONVICTION!

CLARITY

TRUTH OR CONSEQUENCES?

CHAPTER 10

> "ALL WE CAN DO IS
> TO FOLLOW THE
> TRUTH AND NOT
> FIGHT AGAINST IT."
> 2 CORINTHIANS 13:8 CEV

"Little White Lies"
Do they Help or Hurt?

Isn't being truthful ultimately absolute respect for those you touch, for those you love and interact with? Being truthful can often be a daunting and difficult task. It seems so easy to tell a "little white lie" to protect relationships and eliminate arguments.

What do you think of Little White Lies?

CLARITY

So many times, we are pulled toward the easy road of deceit and dishonesty, all the while convincing ourselves that the "Little White Lie" is the best thing to do. By not telling the truth, do we think that we are somehow being kind or saving others pain?

Blurting out the truth in certain situations can hurt. ... It is not always wise to walk into a room and tell your spouse, *"Wow, you're really putting on weight!"* Is it the truth? Maybe. Does it hurt? Probably. Hurting is not born in love. God is love and all that we do that is not out of love, is not of God.

However, being dishonest when your spouse asks if he or she is putting on weight can bring its own hurt. Sometimes the question is a plea for help. Your answer is important in response to a request for loving, truthful advice. Do you hide behind the "White Lie" or do you help?

"HONESTY IS THE FIRST CHAPTER IN THE BOOK OF WISDOM."

Thomas Jefferson

When Jesus said, *"Love your neighbor as yourself"* ~Mark 12:31, wasn't He telling us to put the needs of others above our own, and to treat others as we want to be treated? Is honesty important to you? Do you want people to lie to you? Even small lies?

Hope is the beginning of faith, as giving is a root of Love – truth is at the core of righteousness. Dishonesty, on the other hand, is at the core of all evil and sin. From the Garden of Eden through today, deceit has been used to hurt and destroy loved ones, relationships, nations, and cultures.

So often, dishonesty feels like it can be beneficial. It's not. Are we deceiving ourselves into believing that hiding the truth is an act of love? Will deceit increase happiness, wealth and relieve the stress of the world?

It is during those times when the temptation to deceive is strong, and it is cloaked in benevolence; while looking to be the easy path, we must turn to God for guidance. We need to shun what feels to be rational thinking and logic rattling in our brains; but instead, we must listen to our heart. It is there that we will hear the still, quiet voice of God. His voice will lead us to truth and love – guiding us toward His kingdom in love. After all, don't we usually know the right thing to do?

My first memory of dishonesty was as a young man. It was spring in Iowa, everything had turned green, flowers bloomed, and bees were buzzing. While the changing of the season always heralded the end of school and a summer filled with baseball, swimming and the warmth of the sun; it wouldn't really be summer until the beginning of the St. Theresa Carnival. Every year on Memorial Day, a local Catholic church had a carnival to raise funds for charity. This was the annual event that introduced me to the "Tilt-A-Whirl," "The Scrambler," and my first Ferris wheel ride. Times like that were always full of fun memories with my family. Until that one year.

> For we can do nothing against the truth, but only for the truth.
>
> 2 Corinthians 13:8

Home from school for the holiday, full of anticipation, and barely able to control my enthusiasm. Before our national holidays moved to Mondays creating the 3-day-weekends we all know today, Memorial Day was on the 30th of May.

CLARITY

This year it was Wednesday, giving us Thursday and Friday off school. A five-day weekend! The thought of five days full of rides and carnival arcade games filled my little boy head with happy thoughts.

Waking up early Wednesday morning with enthusiasm usually reserved for Christmas morning, my mom greeted us with breakfast, while Dad was out running some errands.

Getting close to noon, my dad hadn't come home yet. Thinking what could be more important than the carnival? My impatience was almost unbearable. It was my frenzied excitement that led me into my parents' room. Sitting on my dad's dresser was a crisp $10 bill. Without much thought,

> "WHOEVER IS CARELESS WITH THE TRUTH IN SMALL MATTERS CANNOT BE TRUSTED WITH IMPORTANT MATTERS."
>
> Albert Einstein

other than how many rides could be bought with $10; my hand snatched the bill while heading out the door to the carnival by myself. With little thought for my family, the prospect of spending the day in non-stop fun consumed me.

Walking in the door that night was a blur, except for the look on my Dad's face. A face that was typically jovial and full of loving smiles, was now stern with eyes fixed on me. *"Where have you been, Billy?"* he said in his serious voice. Fearing the inevitable scolding, a quick, *"Out with friends"* left my lips. Telling me to sit down he then asked, *"Did you go to the carnival?"*

Trying to cover up my deception by responding, *"No,"* my father answered back with, *"Are you sure?"* He didn't stop there. *"Your brother said he saw you riding rides."* You can probably guess the rest of the conversation. It didn't go well and ended in my full confession filled with tears and sobs. Then came one of the most powerful lessons of my life.

Thinking that my dad was angry about my thieving ways, my head was filled with fear of his punishment. Always kind and understanding, he explained how he had set aside the $10 for our family to go the carnival, and that with my action, we wouldn't be going this year. He went on to tell me that he wasn't going to punish me for taking the money, explaining how seeing my brother and sister's disappointment would be punishment enough.

and you will know the truth, and the truth will make you free.

John 8:32

My first thought was, "phew, no punishment." My relief was shattered with his next words. *"Billy, I can't begin to tell you how disappointed I am in your actions. I understand your excitement for the carnival and the temptation that I left on my dresser."* Then, in a very deep, quiet voice he continued, *"What I can't tolerate is your lying. When I asked you where you were, you should have told me the truth."* With sadness in his eyes, he explained, *"Honesty and truth are the most important things I can teach you. The world is filled with dishonest people and we don't need another one."* With that he told me to go and wait for him in our garage. Gripped in fear and asking, *"The garage? Why the garage?"* His answer still rings in my ears, ... *"Because I don't want anyone to hear you scream."*

CLARITY

My dad and mom were not the spanking kind of parents. In fact, there was only one time my dad spanked me. That day in our garage. He was always a master of discipline. Instead of flying off the handle with anger he would calmly ask questions and explain every step of his punishment.

After waiting for what seemed like hours in the garage and being spanked in my imagination a thousand times, he walked in, took me across his knee and spanked me. The memory of the actual spanking has long since vanished. However, the lessons learned that day are still with me today. Dad's lesson that day planted a seed deep inside that always drove me to be honest and truthful.

> "IT'S DISCOURAGING TO THINK
> HOW MANY PEOPLE ARE
> SHOCKED BY HONESTY AND
> HOW FEW BY DECEIT."
>
> Noël Coward, Blithe Spirit

Throughout my professional life in various companies and corporations, my Christian walk and memories of that day in the garage always led me to be overtly honest – telling the truth, even when it was extremely uncomfortable. The understanding that truth is an act of love, and therefore, came from God, was His guidance for my life; except when it might hurt someone without any clear blessing or benefit. Hurting is not of love.

Through the years, God has always blessed my candor and honesty, not always immediately, sometimes years or decades later. Late in my career, my trustworthiness seemed to open doors to deep relationships with people who typically didn't trust anyone.

Those simple sacrifices of the comfort of a white lie, planted seeds that only God could grasp at the time.

While there are so many examples of God's blessings and favor in my career, one that always comes to mind was my work representing a technology company back in the eighties. The management team decided to hide severe flaw from a new partner that it was my honor to be managing at the time. There was an engineering problem in the design of a new product we were negotiating with our partner.

As it turned out, my company had "bet the farm" on this new technology. If their new partner, a multi-billion dollar, Fortune 500 company found out, most thought they would cancel all launch plans for the product, and probably the partnership. If that happened, my company believed they would go out of business. So, the decision was made to hide the flaw. To their credit, the management team had already developed the plan to fix the problem and were going to provide it to our new partner at no charge.

> Better is open rebuke
> Than love that is
> concealed. Faithful
> are the wounds of
> a friend, But
> deceitful are
> the kisses of
> an enemy.
>
> Proverbs 27:5-6

Unfortunately, the fix would take six months to create and implement in the field. This move would cause untold problems for our partner and more importantly, their customers. There were no plans to resolve those problems, nor compensate the end customer.

After a day full of meetings where the management team emphatically pleaded their case with me, including the threat of termination and extreme retaliation, my heart and head were deep in a battle. The drive home usually took around thirty minutes. On this day, it seemed to take days. All the time knowing the "right" thing to do, my mind bubbled over with the multitude of consequences. How would my family fare? Where would my next job come from? What about all those people at our company?

Aside from the management team, no one knew what was going on, nor had a part in the decision. Still, my decision could put them all out of work. The anxiety was intense. Taking it to God, He reminded me ... *"You already know what to do."*

> ## "IF YOU CAN'T GET RID OF THE SKELETON IN YOUR CLOSET, YOU'D BEST TAKE IT OUT AND TEACH IT TO DANCE."
>
> George Bernard Shaw

There was such peace in that understanding. The knowledge that my decision to be honest with our partner was what God wanted me to do, brought such comfort. Was there fear and doubt? Sure. Knowing that truth was an act of love helped me to keep my fear in check.

That night, calling my customer contact to explain the situation taught me so much about truth, and how God blesses those who sacrifice comfort for righteousness. My contact was calm and understanding. It felt unnatural for a business call of this type. Usually these types of calls were filled with angst, yelling, and threats. Instead, together, we mapped out a plan to work through the issue. No one lost their job; contracts were not canceled, and the partnership remained intact. The launch was simply trimmed back to allow for the fix to be implemented.

As for me, my trust in our management team was obliterated. There was no desire for me to stay with a team that would even consider that kind of action. With God's guidance came the clarity that it was time for a change. Within the next year, God led me to a new company that was undoubtedly the best move of my career.

Two to three years after that phone call, my contact agreed to a million-dollar contract with my new company, simply because of me – he trusted me.

> 'These are the things which you should do: speak the truth to one another; judge with truth and judgment for peace in your gates.
> Zechariah 8:16

That contract led to a business that eventually grew to over $500 million in revenue for his company. God's blessings couldn't have been more obvious: truth in and of itself is its own reward, and honesty will certainly bless your life and career. In my experience, honesty also leads to tangible blessings for all that honor the practice of truth.

CLARITY

"TO BELIEVE IN SOMETHING, AND
NOT TO LIVE IT, IS DISHONEST."

Mahatma Gandhi

165

LOVE In ACTION

THE BEST POLICY

Like most, my life has been full of dishonesty. Not so much my dishonesty, but deceitful practices of colleagues, friends, and loved ones. Not the destructive misleading devious kind of lies. Instead, it seemed people were not truthful in hopes of eliminating pain and friction for me. They believed that their dishonesty was the kind thing to do. Have you experienced benevolent deception? How did it make you feel when you discovered the truth? If you are like me, it made you angry.

Starting with the deceptions of adults, hoping to protect innocent children, followed by dishonesty of my friends, and loved ones, it was usually extremely painful to find out the truth. Pain is pain. No matter if we go through the pain today or years from now. It's still pain.

> Little children, let us not love with word or with tongue, but in deed and truth.
>
> 1 John 3:18

The motivation behind most deception seems to be based in a hope that "they'll never find out." Does that ever work? For me, it seemed the truth would always surface. Often at the worst time. Has that happened to you?

We've all heard the cliché by William Shakespeare, "A coward dies a thousand times before his death, but the valiant taste of death but once. ..." In my experience that was the pain of telling a lie.

The never-ceasing anguish that accompanied my worries of being found out, living the pain of dishonesty every day. Whereas, being honest and going through pain once was so much easier.

Early in my career one of my mentor's taught me a simple management practice that became the core of my "Honesty is the best policy" philosophy.

One day after a major disaster in our company that was the result of someone covering up a problem with a cascade of "white lies," my boss called me into his office. *"Shut the door and have a seat,"* he barked with teeth clenched. Looking him in the eye he had that steam coming out of his ears, bright red face kind of look that told me everything about his

> ## "WE ARE ALL TRAVELERS IN THE WILDERNESS OF THIS WORLD, AND THE BEST WE CAN FIND IN OUR TRAVELS IS AN HONEST FRIEND!"
>
> Robert Louis Stevenson

view of the deception. To his credit, he kept his composure saying, *"Don't you ever do that again!"* Reacting with my finger pointed at the perpetrator of the dishonesty seemed to only magnify his rage. *"I'm not talking about him; I'm talking about you!"* His face seemed to get even more red.

Taking a deep breath, he asked, *"When did you know what was going on?"* Thinking it was a good thing, he heard my explanation. *"We knew last night but we didn't want to ruin your evening, so we decided to tell you this morning."*

LOVE PEOPLE with CONVICTION!

Glaring at me he said, *"In this company, bad news travels fast!"* Continuing, he let me know that he always wanted to be the first to know about a problem. That way, he would never be "broadsided" with an issue, caught in ignorance of what was going on. He finished by explaining how omission of the truth is the same thing as telling a lie. He was clear with me: *"Dishonesty comes in many disguises."* While walking me out of his office he asked for my commitment to always ensure that he was the first person to hear impactful news. Good and bad.

From that day forward, while understanding that omission can be deceitful, it has always been my practice to be overtly honest and truthful in all my relationships without the dishonesty of excluding things known. Sure, there has been a lot of pain, arguing and friction that came with honesty. Nonetheless, it was minuscule in comparison to the pain of a thousand deaths found in the practice of those "little white lies."

LOVE PEOPLE with CONVICTION BY:

"Leading, Loving and Living in Honesty!"

Giving an honest answer
is a sign of true friendship.
Proverbs 24:26 CEV

168

COURAGE

There is No Growth Without Friction

CHAPTER 11

"BUT YOU MUST LEARN TO
ENDURE EVERYTHING, SO
YOU WILL BE COMPLETELY
MATURE AND NOT LACKING
IN ANYTHING."

JAMES 1:4 CEV

Fearful or Faithful?

So many times, it seems we are tangled up in struggles, fearful that we will never see the light of day. Victory is a fleeting hope that fades with every confrontation. Caught in a relentless battle; draining every part of your will to win. A battle that leaves you mired in a puddle of doubt and uncertainty.

Have you been there?

In Christ, we know that when we feel we have nothing left, God is all we need; when we are vulnerable, that's when God picks us up and carries us through. Scripture tells us that with God, all the problems and barriers thrown in our path will fortify us, making us stronger while strengthening our faith. At the same time, God works to build our character, preparing us for challenges and tough times. But even more than that, walking in faith builds our trust in God, while our obedience builds His trust in us.

So, the next time you are overwhelmed with trouble or experiencing hard times, be thankful, and know that with God, you are getting stronger!

> "A SUCCESSFUL MAN IS ONE WHO CAN LAY A FIRM FOUNDATION WITH THE BRICKS OTHERS HAVE THROWN AT HIM."
>
> David Brinkley

GROWTH REQUIRES FRICTION!

Think of how our bodies were created to deal with stress and injury. Getting off the couch, you grab a shovel, and head to the backyard for some gardening. Typically, what is the first thing that happens? Blisters!

Just saying the word brings pain. You work hard all day long to provide some food or added beauty, and what's the result? Your hands and knees are covered in those bubbles just under your skin. If one pops, you know the pain that follows.

In addition to the blisters, the muscles throughout your body feel like you just finished a game of football, and you were the football! Why is that?

You've changed your routine and started using your hands and body for physical labor. Your body is simply protecting you from doing major damage. While the painful blisters and muscles slow you down to begin healing, your body is re-creating itself to endure your new activities in the garden. God never promised there wouldn't be pain. Instead, He designed our bodies to become what we need them to be going forward, to handle the task at hand, enduring the pain. The circumstances of our lives are no different. Sure, there are times when we feel like we can't take one more step; that there is no clear path to a good ending. Like the blisters, it hurts. Sometimes the pain is unbearable.

"Have I not commanded you? Be strong and courageous! Do not tremble or be dismayed, for the LORD your God is with you wherever you go."

Joshua 1:9

In my career there were so many times when it felt as if everything in my life was working against me. Trouble and strife at work would be followed by nights full of family discord and friction. Day after day, night after night, one kick in the teeth followed by a punch in the gut. The conflicts would wear on me until it seemed there was no way to climb out of the muck and mire.

In prayer, God always led me to hang on, but not with immediate answers to prayer. The seas never parted, nor did angels herald my deliverance. Instead, it always felt like God simply had His arm around me saying, *It's going to be okay.*

It is same way my dad would comfort me after losing a ball game. No promise of future victory, no excuses for what happened. Just a simple hug, full of comfort.

For me, that was all it took to not give up. Slowly, my life changed with one small victory after another. God would go to work knocking down barriers and changing hearts. Sometimes the successes were so small, they were hard to see. It was only when looking back at the steps of my life, God shows me His guidance and protection with crystal clear vision.

Through it all, it was those tough times and unbearable experiences when it seemed impossible to hold on, that God created the best parts of my life. Amid all the strife and conflict, my biggest blessings were born.

> "IT TAKES A GREAT DEAL OF BRAVERY TO STAND UP TO OUR ENEMIES, BUT JUST AS MUCH TO STAND UP TO OUR FRIENDS."
>
> J. K. Rowling
> Harry Potter and the Philosopher's Stone

My early years in school were fraught with setbacks and pain. The son of an alcoholic mother with all the baggage that came with that life, and a dad that traveled all the time, my youth was unsupervised. Most would think it was a life of freedom. It wasn't. We all need boundaries and structure, especially as children. It was the lack of structure that took me down some very bumpy roads full of chaos and friction. There is no doubt that the friction experienced in my youth made me strong, independent, and resilient throughout my life.

God always knew where my path would take me, and He always prepared me for each step, protecting me from others and, more importantly, from myself.

The biggest blessing during those days was God's gift of faith. Not the "down on my knees" kind of faith; more of a deep seated belief that things would turn out well. Before knowing much about anything to do with God, my faith was unstoppable. My faith didn't come from books or instruction. Instead, my faith was developed through experience. At an early age, my learning to persevere through adversity grew stronger with each trial or setback. Instead of leaning on my knowledge, or things learned; it was my faith that got me through.

At the time, there was little understanding of God, the Bible, or religion. Instead, it was the feeling of that comforting arm of God around my shoulder that would give me the strength to carry on. So often, when looking back it is easy to see His protection in my life, way before learning anything about Him and His blessings. It was that feeling of comfort that led me through the tough times. The more belief that everything would be all right, the stronger my faith became.

> So we can confidently say, "The Lord is my helper; I will not fear; what can man do to me?
>
> Hebrews 13:6

In multiple training courses throughout my career, we were taught about the "Four Stages of Competence," originally introduced by management trainer Martin M. Broadwell in 1969. The theory would often resurface with various tweaks in the "self-help" book craze of the 1980's and 1990's. In a nutshell, the theory talked about the four stages, or quadrants, of learning.

Unconscious incompetence (you don't know what you don't know), conscious incompetence (you know what you don't know), conscious competence (you know what you know) and unconscious competence (you don't know what you know). During my years in management you would often hear me say, *"Give me a team with only people from the first and fourth quadrant. You can keep the rest."*

In my experience it was the motivated beginners with no knowledge of what to do, that when given a task, would figure out how to get it done. In contrast, it was the people who had been "around the block" with years of experience, reacting through instincts refined in the fires of adversity that would make the best leaders. Leading to the realization that it was the two quadrants that began with "I don't know," that were the most powerful quadrants in the learning cycle. You might be thinking, how can that be? Surely, knowledge is better than instincts or "beginners' luck."

> "SUCCESS IS NOT FINAL;
> FAILURE IS NOT FATAL:
> IT IS THE COURAGE TO
> CONTINUE THAT COUNTS."
>
> Winston S. Churchill

Through the troubled times in my life, it became clear that too much knowledge could get in the way, while faith would carry me through fires that knowledge would not. It took me a while to understand that it was knowledge that drives our fear, always thinking of what could happen and fearing the results could stop me dead in my tracks.

Can you think of any fear you have that is not based in knowledge? If you were sitting in a tall tree looking down at the rocks below, is it a fear of falling that scares you? Or is it your knowledge of gravity and your experiences of the pain when hitting the ground that drives your fear? Is this the innocence of children talked about in scripture? The 'not knowing' about the pain?

The Bible is full of teaching about fear. We are to "fear not" and only believe. Fear is the opposite of faith or belief. In a sense, fear is faith in the bad things that might happen. Things that we conjure up in our thoughts. How often do our fears really happen? Does our anxiety and angst stop bad things from happening? Are we truly more prepared through our worrying? Or does your fear cause you to die a thousand times in your thoughts?

Several years ago, it was God's plan for me to experience brain surgery and the extensive recovery that followed.

> "Be strong and courageous. Do not fear or be in dread of them, for it is the Lord your God who goes with you. He will not leave you or forsake you."
>
> Deuteronomy 31:6

After a God-filled trip to the emergency room at the Mayo Clinic Hospital and a miraculous surgery to remove a brain bleed, it was imperative for me to learn to use my hands and walk again. So, it was off to a rehabilitation/therapy clinic. This was my first time being transported from one medical facility to another by ambulance. The trip helped me realize just how much the surgery had altered my ability to function normally. Simple tasks like walking or using my hands were now an ordeal that needed focus and concentration.

Upon arrival, sitting in the bed that would be my new home for the next few weeks, my thoughts were flooded with questions and concerns. Would my life ever be normal again? Were walkers, wheelchairs, and scooters going to be my new mode of transportation? How would my wife cope with an invalid? Scary is too small a word to describe my anxiety.

COURAGE

Then, the door to my room flew wide open. In walked this kind, but authoritative nurse. Turned out, she wasn't a nurse at all. Announcing that she was the lead therapist on my case she asked, *"What brings you here?"* Scurrying around the room, she proceeded to organize everything near my bed to make it more efficient to get up and move around.

After listening to a brief recap of my story. She walked up to the side of my bed and looked me straight in the eyes. Taking my hand, she said, *"My name is Betty, and don't you worry about a thing. It's my job to make sure you walk out of here as if you never went through surgery. And you should know, I'm pretty good at my job."*

> "YOU CANNOT SWIM
> FOR NEW HORIZONS
> UNTIL YOU HAVE COURAGE
> TO LOSE SIGHT OF THE SHORE."
>
> William Faulkner

It felt like the weight of the world had been lifted off me, allowing me to roll over and sleep like a baby.

Even with all my experiences staying in hotels and hospitals, it was still always a little weird sleeping in a strange bed, especially in a hospital. The next day, still anxious, waking up as the sun was peeking through the shades, while wondering: "What will my first day in rehab be like?"

The door to my room swung open and in with a flood of sunlight walked Betty. *"Good Morning! Are you ready to get out of here yet? We've got a busy day planned for you!"*

In wonder, my first question was, *"How long do you think it'll take to re-train the muscles in my hands and legs?"*

177

"Ha!" she exclaimed with a big grin. *"Rehab got nuttin' to do with your muscles, 'cept maybe the muscle between your ears."* She continued …

"Rehab is all about faith. Faith in your ability to walk, not faith in your muscles." She went on to explain. *"When you sit down, do you think about your butt? Do you focus on how your leg muscles are bending your knees?"* Almost preaching now, she continued, *"Do you even wonder if the chair will hold you? Heck no! You just sit down."*

"That's how you will walk out of this place." Oozing with confidence, she continued. *"When you walk through that door, you're gonna be thinking about hugging your bride and kids, not your next step! Now, let's get started!"*

I say to you, My friends, do not be afraid of those who kill the body and after that have no more that they can do.

Luke 12:4

With my new understanding of the power of faith in things unknown and unseen, it was merely a few weeks later we were saying our goodbyes while walking out the door to hug my wife and kids.

While that experience was horrific on so many levels, it taught me that it is the friction in life that strengthens our faith. Every time we have a victory, small or large, we are emboldened to take a step of faith again. Each time we step in faith, our belief grows. Our faith is strengthened, and we trust that God will cover and protect us. God uses our faith and trust to show us that He loves us and will always be there for us. Like sitting in a chair, eventually our faith becomes a complete and unquestioning trust in God, and His promises. Like those blisters, God gives us what we need to persevere.

178

COURAGE

God knows your pain and like any loving Father, He would do anything to eliminate your agony. Your body uses pain to slow you down while building your new body. In the same way, God will slow you down with the pain and frustrations of life. Not to hurt or punish you, He uses our pain to make us stronger, more resilient. God created us to become stronger and more resilient through tough times. Always remember that we are conquerors and when God is in it, there is no limit. Have faith in God; listen for His still, quiet voice for direction, and persevere!

> ## "COURAGE IS RESISTANCE TO FEAR, MASTERY OF FEAR, NOT ABSENCE OF FEAR."
>
> Mark Twain

There is no victory without first fighting a battle. With God, there is no victory without surrender. That is, surrendering all to God, giving Him your complete and unconditional trust. It is in our full surrender that we find God's Grace and Courage.

COURAGE,

Purified like Silver ...
in the Fires of Surrender & Humility

Strengthened Like Gold ...
in the Furnace of Struggle

Polished Like a Pearl ...
through the Friction & Strife of Life

Love In ACTION

Cowardly Kings

We've all been there. Ready to throw in the towel and quit. After all, defeat wouldn't be so bad, there's always tomorrow. It is what it is, and we can't change it. If there was ever a rallying cry for defeat, those words would be part of the anthem.

My life was full of roadblocks, heartaches, and setbacks. It would be great to tell you how my perseverance carried me through, and that there was never any fear or anxiety in my heart. Well, that wasn't the case. Instead, fear and doubt consumed almost every part of my existence. Especially in those early years. In most cases, it was my ignorance that carried me through the adversity. Looking back, it was the comfort of not knowing what to do that led me to do things that no one had done before. Instead of giving into the desire to give up, you would often hear me say "why not?" Simply said, it was not knowing any better that made things seem possible.

> Therefore, take up the full armor of God, so that you will be able to resist in the evil day, and having done everything, to stand firm.
>
> Ephesians 6:13

During my school days, boys were taught to not show fear. Phrases like, "keep a stiff upper lip" and "big boys don't cry," were clichés handed down from my parents, teachers, and coaches. So, when fear would creep up, it always made me feel inadequate. There must be something wrong with me if my heart was full of fear.

Thankfully, God gave me two role models that would teach all that is needed to be known about fear: The Cowardly Lion and Elvis Presley.

Throughout my childhood, *The Wizard of Oz* was our family Christmas movie. It only got better when we finally got our first color TV. My favorite character in the classic movie was the cowardly lion. He was afraid of everything, including his own tail. Still, he persevered through his fear because of his love and devotion to Dorothy. It was the lion that first taught me that you can be afraid and brave and the same time.

> "I LEARNED THAT COURAGE WAS NOT THE ABSENCE OF FEAR, BUT THE TRIUMPH OVER IT.
>
> THE BRAVE MAN IS NOT HE WHO DOES NOT FEEL AFRAID, BUT HE WHO CONQUERS THAT FEAR."
>
> Nelson Mandela

During the late 60's Elvis made a comeback in hopes of regaining some of his popularity back after we were invaded by Beatlemania. In one of his many interviews during the comeback, a reporter asked him if he still got butterflies in his stomach before going on stage. He answered as only Elvis could. *"Darlin', sure I still get butterflies. Only now, they fly in formation."*

Go figure, the king of the jungle and the King of Rock and Roll were both afraid! They pushed through their fear by focusing on the outcome, not their current circumstance.

It was their faith that carried them through.

Traversing the trials of my life, it was knowing that courage didn't mean fearless, with an understanding that it was okay to be afraid, that brought me through tough times even when fear consumed me.

My resolve didn't develop overnight. Instead, it was a process that was strengthened in the furnace of adversity over years. Much like steel is hardened in a furnace. The more times it is heated in the furnace, the stronger the steel becomes.

There was a day when Elvis was just a scared kid with a dream. Over time, facing his fear with resolve made him stronger each time he stepped on stage. Even when he became an international superstar and the butterflies would start to flutter in his stomach, he would walk out on stage, focusing his butterflies into formation, and knowing that nothing could come between him and his dream.

So, it is in Christ. When we wrap ourselves in His protection, He will carry us through. God never said there wouldn't be fear. Instead we are told to fear not and only believe. For me, fear is usually present in those tough life decisions. All the "What if's about this and that…" Instead of working to eliminate the fear, it is my belief in Christ, and His protection, that gives me power over any fear. Leaning on the power of Christ while telling my butterflies to get in line works for me!

LOVE PEOPLE with CONVICTION BY:

"Being Courageous, Even in Fear!"

The LORD is for me; I will not fear;
What can man do to me?

Psalm 118:6

PASSION

NO WISE MAN CAN REASON AWAY BELIEF

CHAPTER 13

"CHRIST GIVES ME
THE STRENGTH
TO FACE ANYTHING."
Philippians 4:13 CEV

What Fuels Your Life?

When morning sunlight first splashes over your eyes, what are your thoughts? Do you bounce out of bed? Or is your first response to throw the covers over your head and return to dreamland?

What is your Passion?

184

PASSION

Do you wake up knowing what to do, or are your first thoughts *wondering* what to do? Are the desires of your heart a well-lit path or a dim, muddy trail? Is the person you see in the mirror the person you want to be? Or is that person a distant and foggy dream?

You're not alone. Our perception of ourselves is usually quite different than who we are, or how others see us. Most of us hold a deep belief that we can do great things, if only … All the while, we remain unmotivated to move forward on our dreams. Why is that?

> "WE SEE THE WORLD, NOT AS IT IS, BUT AS WE ARE – OR, AS WE ARE CONDITIONED TO SEE IT. WHEN WE OPEN OUR MOUTHS TO DESCRIBE WHAT WE SEE, WE IN EFFECT DESCRIBE OURSELVES, OUR PERCEPTIONS, OUR PARADIGMS. …"
>
> Stephen R. Covey,
> 7 Habits of Highly Effective People

Is it as simple as we're out of fuel? Or worse, we're using diesel fuel in a race car? Sadly, the obstacles in front of us are typically not external barricades or mountains. Often, the obstacles that hold us back are of our own making. Walls built out of one doubt after another: brick by brick.

My relationship with Christ Jesus and the understanding that He would always be with me kept me going through some tough times. Now, looking back at my life, it is easy to see that He not only lit my path going forward, but it was His "living water" that fueled the passion of my life.

Going through so many changes in my career and moving around the country was an energy drain not only for me, but also my family. So many times, the questions outnumbered the answers. Yet, there was that powerful force at the core of my every step. A purpose harboring deep inside of me; a determination to make something of my life. Not so much for me, but for my family. Dropping out of school was an embarrassment. Ultimately, it was the shame and humiliation of my lack of education that fueled my resolve to provide a better life for my bride and our four kids. A determination that was not so clear at the time. The longing to provide a better life for my family was my rocket fuel. It wasn't a desire for me to be a huge success; rather, a need to provide a great life for my family. My focus was never on me or the accolades that would come with achievement. My focus was truly on my family. Dr. Dobson would have been proud.

> I can do all this through him who gives me strength.
>
> Philippians 4:13 NIV

After stating our vows on our wedding day, our deepest desire was to have a loving, caring family, void of the addictions, fighting, and isolation that was rampant in both of our families growing up. Our partnership began with the belief that both of us would work to accomplish our goals, recognizing that the only way out was to be successful. My success was defined by the happiness of my family, not my bank account. Regrettably, the more success in my career, the more time spent away from family. Fortunately, our four kids were in the hands of my beautiful bride. From the first day we met, her "Golden Heart" shined on everyone we knew. Thankfully, all of our kids inherited and adopted her heart of unconditional love. Over time, the determination in my heart to provide for my family became the momentum that fueled my every step. My passion.

Passion

Most times, it didn't feel like something special. What is now known as my passion was often misconstrued as stubbornness and pride. So many times, my desire to be humble would stifle my drive and enthusiasm. This made seeing the passion to succeed as a weakness, not a strength.

Most of the people around me worked extremely hard not to work. It was puzzling to see them hatching elaborate plans to reduce their workload. In a sense, all their energy was spent on not using energy. So many times, their disagreements over their workload with peers turned into all out battles and feuds. If they would have just focused that energy on getting the job done, think of what they could have accomplished.

> "A SMALL DAILY TASK,
> IF IT BE REALLY DAILY,
> WILL BEAT THE LABOURS
> OF A SPASMODIC HERCULES."
>
> Anthony Trollope

While my approach was typically not the most cunning, using love and perseverance seemed to outlast everyone, resulting in little interference. Love is the true insurmountable force in the universe. Over time, love and perseverance became the vehicle for my passion. Powered with empathy, while leading with love and driving through the struggles with persistence and stubbornness.

It might surprise you that the word passion is a derivative of the Greek word "pati," which means to endure or suffer. In Christ we use it to define Christ's suffering from the Garden of Gethsemane, to the cross on Calvary, "The Passion of Christ." On his trip from the Garden to the Cross, Christ showed us how to persevere through suffering in the name of love.

Looking back at my life and career, it is clear how God used my passion for my family to fuel my accomplishments, leading me through suffering with love and endurance.

My passion led me down countless paths, including one late night in a lonely "sky-bridge" in Boston. The sky-bridge connected the convention center to a classic downtown Marriott hotel. A welcomed pathway on a frigid February night. Below the bridge was one of the busiest intersections in Boston. Day or night, traffic buzzed up and down the six-lane roads below. Replicating the hotel's decor, the pathway was beautiful. Wall-to-wall tile covered the immense walkway that seemed to be several blocks long.

The length of the walkway made it formidable. The warm, sheltered pathway from the hotel to the convention center was usually traveled in the mornings with conventioneers scurrying to change the world with a fresh start every morning. In contrast, it was always a tough hike back to the hotel after a long day of standing on concrete floors. Such was the case this late Sunday evening.

> Never give up. Eagerly follow the Holy Spirit and serve the Lord.
> **Romans 12:11 CEV**

After a busy day setting up the trade show booth in preparation for the "Big Show" opening on Monday morning, it was finally time to head back to a warm bed to rest my feet. At eleven o'clock on a Sunday night, the walkway was completely empty. Even the traffic below was gone. The only sound was the loud echoes of my dress shoes on the hard tile. In the middle of my trek, the rhythmic clicks of my heels were interrupted by another set of heel clicks echoing from the other side of the bridge. Some poor soul heading back to the convention center on this late Sunday night.

PASSION

Entering the end of the long corridor, to my astonishment, was Kevin James, one of the sales stars on my team from a job two companies ago. Both of us, walking faster with ear to ear smiles, shouting, *"What are you doing here?"* How funny it was that of all the places in the world, two colleagues from Minneapolis would meet in an empty walkway in Boston so late on a cold Sunday night!

After catching up and chuckling about running into each other so far from home, the conversation turned to my reasons for being there, and my quest to find a new job. We talked about how a week prior to the show's start, the parent company of my employer, a small startup in the wide format printing space had pulled the plug on our operation. The abrupt end to the company meant there was no support for a trade show almost 1500 miles away.

"REJECT YOUR SENSE OF INJURY, AND THE INJURY ITSELF DISAPPEARS"

Marcus Aurelius "the Philosopher King"

We were asked to stay on for a couple of weeks to oversee the dismantling of the company. Normally, that would have been it, close everything down, and spend the time to go and look for a new position.

Nevertheless, this shutdown was anything but normal. All the show's expenses were contracted to be paid by our partners in London. In agreement with them, all we needed to do was provide people to man the booth, with our company paying travel and expenses. If it had been our company on the contracts, we could have just walked away.

However, since it was in our partners' name, and they weren't closing, they would need to pay the bill, show or no show.

Over the past year, while working with the two principals of the company in London, they had become good friends and trusted colleagues. The two were typical, proper Brits. Polite, punctual, and proud. The guy who ran the business, Teddy, could have played a British butler in the movies. Their lead software engineer, Lizzy, was a gruff, crass, and argumentative middle-aged woman who looked as if she would have been more at home on a Harley than sitting behind a computer. To have the two in the same meeting was as informative as it was entertaining.

Talking by phone, Teddy and Lizzy were devastated by the news of our company's closing. Rightly so, their concerns quickly fell on paying for a booth with no one in it, except

> Let us not lose heart in doing good, for in due time we will reap if we do not grow weary.
>
> Galatians 6:9

for the two of them. They went on to explain how their travel expenses were all non-refundable; clearly, the result of Teddy's frugal budgeting.

After hearing my story of woe, Kevin said, *"You should stop by the booth and meet my boss, Bob, you two would be great together. He might even offer you a job and we could sure use your help."* Listening to details of my predicament was probably not how Kevin wanted to spend the rest of his Sunday night, so that was the extent of the unplanned rendezvous. We both agreed how great it was to see each other and that we would talk more at his booth. At that, we bid each other adieu.

Well, as dog-tired as one could be, sleep still eluded me throughout the night. Before long, the phone was ringing with its "Get outta bed" fanfare. Time to wake up and get into the shower to make it to the booth by 8:00 a.m.

Working to get everything up and running in the booth got me wondering about Kevin's boss. What kind of guy is he and why is his company so unknown? The show doors opened at 10 a.m. and the usual anxious attendees began to flood into the convention center.

> ## "THE TRUE SOLDIER FIGHTS NOT BECAUSE HE HATES WHAT IS IN FRONT OF HIM, BUT BECAUSE HE LOVES WHAT IS BEHIND HIM."
>
> GK Chesterton

This was my first time running a booth alone. It kept me darting around the booth, answering as many questions as possible. Apprehension was creeping in, hoping for some reinforcements in the form of Teddy and Lizzy. Finally, around 2 p.m. there they were, Teddy looking his proper self and Lizzy grumbling about all their travel woes, thanks mostly to Teddy. Their banter back and forth was my cue to excuse myself long enough to grab some lunch and stop by Kevin's booth to meet his boss.

Trade show food is just about the worst thing you can eat. Second only to school lunches. Usually prepared the day before, everything at a trade show usually tastes like the cardboard containers it is served in. One of my many "tricks of the trade" learned from countless conventions was to never eat anything at a trade show that comes from an animal. It was usually the hamburgers, hot dogs, tacos or cheese that brought on the "trade show flu." So, after a gourmet meal of a pretzel and French fries, it was off to meet Kevin's boss, all the while wondering, "Would this be it? My new job?"

Is Our Perception Our Reality?

The human condition can be a struggle. We often only see the world that we want to see. Why is that? It's not unlike driving a car. If not for the rear view and side mirrors, we would only see the path in front of us. Have you ever tried to drive a car without mirrors? Or worse, have you ever tried to drive backwards while facing forward? How did it make you feel? Our ability to comprehend our world is limited by our understanding, or our perception of our surroundings. Driving backwards takes us out of our perceived situation, making us uncomfortable to say the least. What if, like my mom, you had eyes in the back of your head? Wouldn't driving backwards be a cinch?

> Watch over your heart with all diligence, For from it flow the springs of life.
>
> Proverbs 4:23

It is that understanding that led me to always be aware of my focus more than my situation. Driving backwards is made simple once we change our focus and work within that perspective.

In his landmark book, *The Seven Habits of Highly Effective People*, Stephen Covey uses a graphic illustration to make his point about perspective. When looking at the drawing, some see an elderly lady with a scowling face accented by a large nose, while others see a fashionably dressed beautiful young woman. How can that be? Perception.

Curiously, once you know about both women in the picture, you can choose which one you see by changing your perspective. Like seeing one woman or the other, is our perception of our life as simple as what we choose to see?

In the animated film, *The Point*, one of my favorite singer/ songwriters from the seventies, Harry Nilsson, teaches us about perspective. If you know the story, you know of the main character, a young boy named Oblio, and his quest in search of a point in the "pointless" forest. It's one of my all-time favorite children's stories. On his adventure through the forest, Oblio meets "Rock Man," who explains to Oblio, *"There is nothing 'pointless' about the Pointless Forest. In fact,"* the Rock Man continues, *"All the trees have points, and the leaves have points, …"* Leaving Oblio with a lot to ponder, the Rock Man tells him, *"You see what you want to see, and you hear what you want to hear."*

> "COLOR IS MY
> DAY-LONG OBSESSION,
> JOY AND TORMENT."
>
> Claude Monet

In a sense, it's not about the reality of the forest, but Oblio's perception of the forest. Such is the human condition. When we believe our life is pointless, it is our job to find the point of our life, not to wait around until our point finds us.

Until meeting Kevin in that quiet walkway, my trip to Boston certainly seemed pointless. Would it really lead me to my next job? Now, walking over to meet Kevin's boss seemed more about a path to my destiny than a walk in the Pointless Forest. Thinking to myself, "What are the odds of running into Kevin 1500 miles from home? This has to be my destiny!" And just like that, my perspective changed.

Walking into the booth, Kevin was nowhere to be found. Coming toward me from across the booth was a tall, thin, red-haired young man with a huge smile. Extending his hand in welcome, he said, *"You must be Mark?"* Shaking hands, he went on to say, *"My name is Bob, and Kevin has been talking about you all day. I'm glad we have a chance to meet."* Explaining that Kevin was deep in conversation with a customer, Bob asked me to go grab a cup of coffee with him.

Do you remember what it was like when you met your best friend for the first time? That's how it felt with Bob and me. We were kindred spirits. Both of us loved the potential of technology and how it could solve problems. Telling one "war story" after another, our casual conversation went on for hours. Parting ways when the show was closing for the day, Bob insisted that we keep in touch and that he would love for me to join their company.

> Do your work willingly, as though you were serving the Lord himself, and not just your earthly master.
>
> Colossians 3:23 CEV

After joining Kevin and Bob's company back in Minneapolis and getting to know Bob better, it became clear that his motivation revolved around providing for his family - much like me. While Bob was immensely competitive and a shrewd strategist, he was doing it all for his family, not for accolades or wealth. Understanding his motivation pulled us closer together. Watching Bob every day, and how his success came through his passion for his family, changed my outlook and my life, including my perspective. It was that job and my relationship with Bob that led me to define the rest of my career with the understanding that my passion *was* my family.

After chasing my career around the country, with over fifteen jobs, living in seven different states, some would say there was no focus in my life or career. After all, what could sustain someone through all the change and adversity? You might think that the chaos was devastating. It was. Particularly in the early years when our kids were young, and the money was scarce. The one constant in my career was my positive outlook: an unquenchable thirst to have a better day today than yesterday.

In the beginning, the early years of my career were spent in fear of failure (FOF), thinking how one mistake would bring everything crashing down. In a sense, it was that fear that drove my actions. However, looking back after my retirement, my motivation is now crystal clear. Implementing the

> "DESIRE IS THE KEY
> TO MOTIVATION,
> BUT IT'S DETERMINATION
> AND COMMITMENT TO
> AN UNRELENTING
> PURSUIT OF YOUR GOAL
>
> A COMMITMENT TO EXCELLENCE
> THAT WILL ENABLE YOU
> TO ATTAIN
> THE SUCCESS YOU SEEK."
>
> Mario Andretti

lesson learned from Bob that it was my passion to provide for my family got me out of bed every day. A passion that drove every step of my career. My passion was simply that, to give my family a better life.

So often, we hear of people driven to success say, "I'm doing it for my family." No doubt a lot of them are. Like me, God will bless their loving passion. Nevertheless, there are those who are driven by the things of the world, thinking it's for their family. Scripture tells us to guard our hearts above all else, for everything we do flows from our heart. It is the passion in our heart that drives us. If our desire is getting that fast car or extra-big house, aren't we focused on the things of this world? Things that only money can buy? Some people get too wrapped up in the money, but like Lennon and McCartney of the Beatles sang, "Money Can't Buy Me Love."

We are repeatedly warned in scripture about the love of money and the evil it can bring. For it is what we treasure that inspires us. It always helps me to ask myself these questions: "What is my real motivation? Is it the latest shiny object that everyone will notice? Or is it that intangible act of love that no one will notice? Which one would Christ want me to choose?"

So many times in my life when choosing the unnoticeable act of love, God has showered me and my family with blessings. After all, with God, it always comes down to our choice. That's why He blessed us with free will. Not so we can do what we want to do. Instead, we choose freely to do the right thing and to listen to God's voice inside each of us. Choosing an act of love will bless us long after the treasures of this world have turned to dust.

> He who loves money will not be satisfied with money, nor he who loves abundance with its income. This too is vanity.
>
> Ecclesiastes 5:10

PASSION

"THE QUALITY OF A PERSON'S
LIFE IS IN DIRECT PROPORTION
TO THEIR COMMITMENT TO
EXCELLENCE, REGARDLESS
OF THEIR CHOSEN
FIELD OF ENDEAVOR."

Vince Lombardi

LOVE IN ACTION

WHAT YOU SEE, IS WHAT YOU GET

So often, when the world seems to be crashing down around us, we feel helpless and abandoned. *If only others could see the world and its destruction like me.* Doesn't it seem that those are the times we want to give up, throw in the towel? If only we could find someone, anyone, to agree with our view of the world. Would there be comfort in knowing that someone was as unhappy as me?

Sadly, a lot of us live our lives in that world. Seeing only what is wrong. Every day it seems people "are out to get us." We live in a corrupt and greedy world that is unjust and unfair, wondering, "Do others recognize the injustice of how some people act? They must see the inequality."

> For the love of money is a root of all sorts of evil, and some by longing for it have wandered away from the faith and pierced themselves with many griefs.
>
> 1 Timothy 6:10

Growing up in an alcoholic family, every conversation seemed to be about what the world was doing to us. If not management at work, then the government or the kids at school. One version of "They-are-always-out-to-get-us" after another, filled every evening; as they succumbed to their woes, one drink at a time. The slurs of intolerance against anything and everything turned into loud rants in opposition of the oppressors. Sometimes the rants would turn to rage. Often, the sedating effects of alcohol would stifle the protest in a haze of slumber. In most cases, all was forgotten the next morning.

PASSION

The fervent protests from a few hours earlier would give way to the chaos of the morning preparation of life, only to start the cycle all over again that night.

From my earliest memory to the freedom of adulthood, it was always the same. Sure, the players and circumstances would change, but the cycle of complaint was persistent through the last decade of my youth.

Leaving home and spending time with the love of my life resulted in something wonderful. The world changed! No longer was it the cynical, hateful place with everyone out to get me. Now, the world seemed beautiful and everyone we met were kind and loving. How could that be?

"LIFE IS 10% WHAT YOU MAKE IT, 90% HOW YOU TAKE IT

Irving Berlin

We would literally walk around with a smile on our face while thinking of all the possibilities. The difference was so stark, it seemed that we must have moved into an alternate universe. Gone were the hatred, vitriol and strife of my home. It had all been replaced with universal love and caring. It was only when going home to visit my family, that everything began to make sense.

That hateful world was still there. It was my perspective that had changed. My new universe was now filled with love flowing out of my relationship with Christ Jesus and my soon-to-be bride. Learning that it was my choice which universe to live in.

My choice of perception didn't change the reality of the world. Sadly, all the hate and vitriol were still there. As Christ taught, the Kingdom of God is at hand. It is our choice if we want to be of the Kingdom of God or the Kingdom of Darkness. You might be thinking that seeing the world through "rose colored glasses" isn't reality. In my experience, what you see IS what you get. If you see the world through muddy glasses, your vision is cloudy.

Like choosing to see the grumpy old lady or the beautiful young woman in the picture, it is our choice of what we see and what our world looks like.

Which kingdom do you see?

LOVE PEOPLE with CONVICTION BY:
"Seeing the World Through the Eyes of God!"

And we know that God causes
all things to work together for good
to those who love God,
to those who are called
according to His purpose.

Romans 8:28

"LOVE IS THE ANSWER. ...
... WHAT WAS THE QUESTION?"

John Lennon

AND, IN THE END ...

Today finds me retired with four wonderful adult children, three grandsons, and still married to the love of my life. You might be thinking, "some guys have all the luck!" If my dad were still around, he would tell you, "There is no such thing as luck!" His definition of luck was when opportunity and preparedness meet.

Throughout my career, being blessed with an insatiable work ethic and an unlimited imagination always kept me prepared. For over four decades in corporate jobs, as an Un-Churched, Un-Bibled, and Un-Hymned child of God striving to meet most challenges and people with unconditional love. God has blessed me with an abundance of opportunity. It is only through the love of God, His blessings of protection, courage, and passion that this high school dropout could find so much joy. Joy that didn't come from possessions or accolades. Instead, the joy of my family and walking hand-in-hand with Christ Jesus; living to glorify Him in all things.

At the end of my career, my health forced me to retire early. No, it isn't a story of me and my bride riding into the sunset. Instead, my ego and selfishness took over. After so many years of focusing on God and others, my bad health consumed me, leading me to concentrate on only me. Looking back, it is easy to see what drove me into a self-indulged "pity party." It was all about focus. By fixing my thoughts on my situation, my bad health and everything that had happened; my sadness and depression grew exponentially. It was only the love of God that pulled me out of the muck and mire that had engulfed me.

After my career was over, it was God's grace and favor that took me through the toughest years of my life, delivering me to a life full of joy. A life focused on loving God and loving people. To think God had brought me full circle, back to His un-conditional gift of love that started so many years ago is a blessing. It was that understanding that led me to look at my life and begin to realize that all the years were about love. Love was in my genes; it was a true gift from God to be born in the generation known for eternity as the "love generation."

Throughout our history, there have been so many remarkable generations we remember and honor. The generations that profoundly changed the world. There were the pilgrims and explorers that traversed an unknown ocean in search of religious and individual freedoms. Recently celebrating the 75th anniversary of D-Day, paying tribute to the "Greatest Generation" that saved us all from the dictatorial tyranny that was choking the nations of the world.

My generation was not as noticeable as the one that saw 175,000 troops hit the beaches of Normandy to liberate Europe. Still, the "Love Generation" changed the world. Our flag bearers were not soldiers with guns; we had four lads from Liverpool with long hair and guitars: The Beatles!

From their first big hit, "Love Me Do," to the last song on their last album, "The End," John, Paul, George and Ringo consistently taught our generation to lead with love. At the end of their landmark last album, Abbey Road, all four voices rang out the battle cry that would guide our generation, "And in the end, the love you take, is equal to the love, you make." Clearly biblical in its message.

Throughout my life, God has blessed me with the understanding that He can guide us through so many different sources. It is our choice whether we look for God in all things. He is always there. Music has been a catalyst for me. Growing closer to God each day, He would teach and guide me through everything in my path including Rock & Roll. Such was my lesson about love that started before the age of ten, and still guides every step of my life today.

Maybe "Leading with Love" is new to you. (Or you are a follower of Christ Jesus, but not focused on **Love** as the core of your relationship with God, or each other). Perhaps, Love is essential in your walk in Christ. In all cases, let us rejoice and glorify God, for touching our hearts with His wonderful message of Agape Love.

Like a lot of you, for most of my life, when asked what my beliefs were, my response would always be, "I'm a Christian, a child of God!" Regrettably, my walk did not match my talk. While my heart was usually in the right place, my brain guided my life. It was MY obedience to analysis and MY planning that drove MY actions. It was MY relentless study, worry and strategies that frequently led me off course. Giving into MY desires for things of the world led me down some very dark roads.

Thankfully, God gave me an intense stubborn streak. You would often hear me say, "My way or the highway!" It was my stubbornness that kept me focused on God's two great commandments, "Love God & Love People." Not always understanding the power God had given me, it is now easier to appreciate why and how He led me through life.

One of my favorite teachers, Dr. Robert Schuller, taught in his message, "Oh, That's Where the Road Leads!" that it is often difficult to see the hand of God in our current situation. Dr. Schuller explained how it is easier to see God working in our lives in retrospect, looking back to see God's Blessings, through His footsteps in the sand. Like counting goldfish in a bowl. If you are in the bowl, it is almost impossible to count the fish as they scurry about. However, the task of counting fish is simple from outside the bowl.

After a life full of love and God's abundant blessings, at the end of my career, the things of the world grabbed hold of me, instead of going to God, my attention turned solely on me while still believing in my salvation through Christ Jesus. Relying on MY own understanding and abilities led me to begin drinking again, after thirty years of sobriety. There was comfort in the escape that comes with alcohol while taking opioids for chronic back pain. With that combination, it didn't take long to add medical marijuana back into the mix. It was easy to rationalize the necessity of self-medication to relieve pain and find comfort.

Looking back, it is easy to see how my reliance on things of the world was not bringing relief; rather, it brought more pain, anxiousness, and sorrow. After a while, noticing the devastation around me, it was obvious that it was all MY doing. Time and again, trying to stop, only led me deeper into my addictions and depression. Even the year that saw me go through heart failure, along with major brain and back surgeries, didn't give me a reason to stop. If anything, that year seemed to take me further into my grief. All the while thinking of only me. Never before had the "Oh Woe is Me" thinking have such a grip on everything in my life.

It was only the risk of losing my beautiful bride that finally got my attention. After forty-plus years of marriage, she was done. Letting me know that she loved me but could not stand by and watch me kill myself, she was leaving. It was the fear of losing the love of my life that lead me to my knees in an ocean of tears and regret.

On that morning, in prayer, my Savior, Christ Jesus, pulled me out my addictions and set me on His Solid Rock. It was that morning, on my knees, that my focus was lifted off me when surrendering everything to Christ Jesus.

From that moment forward, He has helped me to grow closer to Him and by His promise, He has grown closer to me.

After my unconditional surrender, the next few years were spent in constant prayer, meditation, and instruction in His Word; all guided by the Holy Spirit in union with Christ. It is in my walk with God that He has shown me three simple principles that guide my life today, keeping me fully focused on Him 100% of the time. My corporate and marketing background led me to adopt a simple acronym to keep these principles in the forefront of all my thoughts, "S.O.P." Some might recognize this as "Standard Operating Procedure." But that is not what my acronym means; for me, it is all about **Surrender, Obedience and Patience. S.O.P.**

SURRENDER is more than just giving up. When we submit in surrender, we give up all that we are, holding on to nothing of our life or the things of the world. When we consider surrender, we often think of white flags or "hands in the air," the internationally known act of surrender. Raised hands is also the internationally known act of victory. When we surrender to Christ Jesus, with complete submission to God's will, He blesses us with Complete Victory!

OBEDIENCE was, and is, the hardest lesson for me. Most of my life had been spent being obedient to MY thoughts and MY understanding. It didn't take long to understand that my Submissive Surrender to God meant complete obedience as well. How does that work? What are the rules and guidelines? Was my new path all about listening to teachers, reading scripture while listening for the still voice inside me? Was that "God's Will?" It was just that simple. Albeit with one divine requirement; to do all these things, "in Christ."

For, in Christ, we are guided by the Holy Spirit, God's promise of truth that brings the peace that surpasses all understanding through our Obedience.

PATIENCE is a virtue, right? Most of my life was without that virtue. Instead, impatience guided most of my steps. Always seeking MY answers and rewards instantly created dissatisfaction in most situations. If it didn't happen in MY time frame, successful or not, it was not viewed as a victory. Still impatient while surrendering to God, and being Obedient, wondering why my prayers weren't being answered. **Right now!**

It was only when looking back at my life, that God helped me to see the Power of Patience, finding the peace that comes with the gift of patience in union with Christ.

In Christ, we know that patience is a Fruit of the Spirit. As Apostle Paul teaches in Galatians 5:22-23," ...patience, as well as all the virtues of the fruit, are gifts from God." So, where do we find patience? Is it something that we can learn? Teach ourselves? No.

Patience is a gift, not something we create nor can we control. Patience comes only as a gift in our loving relationship with Christ Jesus through the Holy Spirit. When we love God and others, taking the focus off of ourselves, we find the gift of Patience.

After so many years of working to figure things out on my own, God led me to understand that all the parts of the Fruit of the Spirit are born in Love. To find patience, lead with Love. As in all things, love is the answer. Love God & Love People!

When it is difficult to find patience, or any of God's gifts, His word tells us that everything we do, should be done in Love. It is in our acts of Love that God blesses us with the Fruit of the Spirit. When acting in Love of God, or others, our eyes are no longer centered on ourselves nor the things of the world. When our focus is not on ourselves, we find victory in those simple two Great commandments...

Love God with All Your Heart, Soul and Mind,

and Love Others as We Love Ourselves.

"If you love each other, everyone will know that you are my disciples."

John 13:35 CEV

Love is more important
than anything else. It
is what ties everything
completely together.

Colossians 3:14 CEV

Scripture References

SECTION HEADING SCRIPTURES:

1. So love the LORD your God with all your heart, soul, and strength. – Deuteronomy 6:5 CEV
2. For everything created by God is good, and nothing is to be rejected if it is received with gratitude; – 1 Timothy 4:4 NAS
3. Be kind and compassionate to one another, forgiving each other, just as in Christ God forgave you. – Ephesians 4:32 NIV
4. I appeal to you, brothers, in the name of our Lord Jesus Christ, that all of you agree together, so that there may be no divisions among you and that you may be united in mind and conviction. – 1 Corinthians 1:10 BST

CHAPTER HEADING SCRIPTURES:

1. We must hold tightly to the hope we say is ours. After all, we can trust the one who made the agreement with us. – Hebrews 10:23 CEV
2. With all your heart you must trust the LORD and not your own judgment. – Proverbs 3:5 CEV
3. That I may proclaim with the voice of thanksgiving And declare all Your wonders. – Psalm 26:7 NAS
4. Never let go of loyalty and faithfulness. Tie them around your neck; write them on your heart. – Proverbs 3:3 GNT
5. This is why you must encourage and help each other, just as you are already doing. – 1 Thessalonians 5:11 CEV
6. Remember this saying, A few seeds make a small harvest, but a lot of seeds make a big harvest. – 2 Corinthian 9:6 CEV
7. Whoever is the greatest should be the servant of the others. – Matthew 23:11 CEV
8. And the peace of God, which surpasses all understanding, will guard your hearts and minds in Christ Jesus. – Philippians 4:7 NAS
9. Love each other as brothers and sisters and honor others more than you do yourself. – Romans 12:10 CEV
10. All we can do is to follow the truth and not fight against it. – 2 Corinthians 13:8 CEV
11. But you must learn to endure everything, so you will be completely mature and not lacking in anything. – James 1:4 CEV
12. Christ gives me the strength to face anything. – Philippians 4:13 CEV

NOTE: All scriptures are New American Standard translation unless noted.

Scripture References

CHAPTER SCRIPTURES:

Chapter #1 – Faith

But seek first His kingdom and His righteousness, and all these things will be added to you. ... – Matthew 6:33

With all your heart you must trust the LORD and not your own judgment. – Proverbs 3:5 CEV

And without faith it is impossible to please Him, For he who comes to God must believe that He is and that He is a rewarder of those who seek Him. – Hebrews 11:6

Jesus called for a child to come over and stand near him. Then he said: I promise you this. If you don't change and become like a child, you will never get into the kingdom of heaven. – Matthew 18:2-3 CEV

Chapter #2 – Focus

For as he thinks within himself, so he is. He says to you, Eat and drink! But his heart is not with you. – Proverbs 23:7

Looking at them, Jesus said, With people it is impossible, but not with God; for all things are possible with God. – Mark 10:27

Seek the LORD and His strength; Seek His face continually. – 1 Chronicles 16:11

For the mind set on the flesh is death, but the mind set on the Spirit is life and peace, – Romans 8:6

Therefore we also, since we are surrounded by so great a cloud of witnesses, let us lay aside every weight, and the sin which so easily ensnares us, and let us run with endurance the race that is set before us, fixing our eyes on Jesus, the author and perfecter of faith, who for the joy set before Him endured the cross, despising the shame, and has sat down at the right hand of the throne of God. – Hebrews 12:1-2

NOTE: All scriptures are New American Standard translation unless noted.

Scripture References

Chapter #3 – Gratitude

Be anxious for nothing, but in everything by prayer and supplication with thanksgiving let your requests be made known to God. – Philippians 4:6

Let us come before His presence with thanksgiving, let us shout joyfully to Him with psalms. – Psalm 95:2

That I may proclaim with the voice of thanksgiving and declare all Your wonders. – Psalm 26:7

Enter His gates with thanksgiving And His courts with praise. Give thanks to Him, bless His name. – Psalm 100:4

but thanks be to God, who gives us the victory through our Lord Jesus Christ. – 1 Corinthians 15:57

Let the peace of Christ rule in your hearts, to which indeed you were called in one body; and be thankful. – Colossians 3:15

But thanks be to God, who always leads us in triumph in Christ, and manifests through us the sweet aroma of the knowledge of Him in every place. – 2 Corinthians 2:14

giving thanks to the Father, who has qualified us to share in the inheritance of the saints in Light. – Colossians 1:12

Devote yourselves to prayer, keeping alert in it with an attitude of thanksgiving; – Colossians 4:2

And in that day you will say, Give thanks to the LORD, call on His name. Make known His deeds among the peoples; Make them remember that His name is exalted. – Isaiah 12:4

NOTE: All scriptures are New American Standard translation unless noted.

CHAPTER SCRIPTURES: *continued ...*

Chapter #4 – Devotion

A wicked messenger falls into adversity, But a faithful envoy brings healing. – Proverbs 13:17

Therefore, those also who suffer according to the will of God shall entrust their souls to a faithful Creator in doing what is right. – 1 Peter 4:19

Love one another warmly as Christians and be eager to show respect for one another. – Romans 12:10 GNT

But store up for yourselves treasures in heaven, where neither moth nor rust destroys, and where thieves do not break in or steal; for where your treasure is, there your heart will be also. ... – Matthew 6:20-21

Chapter #5 – Encouragement

We should keep on encouraging each other to be thoughtful and to do helpful things. – Hebrews 10:24 CEV

You obey the law of Christ when you offer each other a helping hand. – Galatians 6:2 CEV

Let your light shine before men in such a way that they may see your good works, and glorify your Father who is in heaven. – Matthew 5:16

But exhort one another every day, as long as it is called today, that none of you may be hardened by the deceitfulness of sin. – Hebrews 3:13

A new commandment I give to you, that you love one another, even as I have loved you, that you also love one another. – John 13:34

Love each other as brothers and sisters and honor others more than you do yourself. – Romans 12:10 CEV

And looking at them Jesus said to them, With people this is impossible, but with God all things are possible. – Matthew 19:26

NOTE: All scriptures are New American Standard translation unless noted.

Scripture References

CHAPTER SCRIPTURES: *continued ...*

Chapter #6 – Awareness

For the entire law is fulfilled in keeping this one command: Love your neighbor as yourself. – Galatians 5:14 NIV

Do nothing from selfishness or empty conceit, but with humility of mind regard one another as more important than yourselves; – Philippians 2:3

Finally, all of you should agree and have concern and love for each other. You should also be kind and humble. – 1 Peter 3:8 CEV

Be completely humble and gentle; be patient, bearing with one another in love. – Ephesians 4:2 NIV

Therefore encourage one another and build one another up, just as you are doing. – Thessalonians 5:11

God has given each of you a gift from his great variety of spiritual gifts. Use them well to serve one another. – 1 Peter 4:10 NLT

Chapter #7 – Empathy

Be kind to one another, tender-hearted, forgiving each other, just as God in Christ also has forgiven you. – Ephesians 4:32

Blessed are the merciful, for they shall receive mercy. – Matthew 5:7

Remember the prisoners, as though in prison with them, and those who are ill-treated, since you yourselves also are in the body. – Hebrews 13:3

Help carry one another's burdens, and in this way you will obey the law of Christ. – Galatians 6:2 GNT

Love one another warmly as Christians and be eager to show respect for one another. – Romans 12:10 GNT

Be of the same mind toward one another; do not be haughty in mind, but associate with the lowly. Do not Be wise in your own estimation· – Romans 12:16

God is always fair. He will remember how you helped his people in the past and how you are still helping them. You belong to God, and he won't forget the love you have shown his people. – Hebrews 6:10 CEV

NOTE: All scriptures are New American Standard translation unless noted.

CHAPTER SCRIPTURES: *continued ...*

Chapter #8 – Understanding

A friend loves at all times, And a brother is born for adversity. – Proverbs 17:17

If a kingdom is divided against itself, that kingdom cannot stand. If a house is divided against itself, that house will not be able to stand. – Mark 3:24-25

Do not judge, and you will not be judged; and do not condemn, and you will not be condemned; pardon, and you will be pardoned. – Luke 6:37

Let all bitterness and wrath and anger and clamor and slander be put away from you, along with all malice. – Ephesians 4:31

Pride goes before destruction, a haughty spirit before a fall. – Proverbs 16:18 NIV

Treat others just as you want to be treated. – Luke 6:31 CEV

What the gnawing locust has left, the swarming locust has eaten; And what the swarming locust has left, the creeping locust has eaten; And what the creeping locust has left, the stripping locust has eaten. – Joel 1:4

Let no one look down on your youthfulness, but rather in speech, conduct, love, faith and purity, show yourself an example of those who believe, – 1 Timothy 4:12

Chapter #9 – Trust

Be devoted to one another in love. Honor one another above yourselves. – Romans 12:10 NIV

The king is the friend of all who are sincere and speak with kindness. – Proverbs 22:11 CEV

A friend loves at all times, And a brother is born for adversity. – Proverbs 17:17

The righteous is a guide to his neighbor, But the way of the wicked leads them astray. – Proverbs 12:26

Iron sharpens iron, So one man sharpens another. – Proverbs 27:17

NOTE: All scriptures are New American Standard translation unless noted.

Scripture References

CHAPTER SCRIPTURES: *continued ...*

Chapter #10 – Clarity

For we can do nothing against the truth, but only for the truth. – 2 Corinthians 13:8

and you will know the truth, and the truth will make you free. – John 8:32

Better is open rebuke Than love that is concealed. Faithful are the wounds of a friend, But deceitful are the kisses of an enemy. – Proverbs 27:5-6

These are the things which you should do: speak the truth to one another; judge with truth and judgment for peace in your gates. – Zechariah 8:16

Little children, let us not love with word or with tongue, but in deed and truth. – 1 John 3:18

Giving an honest answer is a sign of true friendship. – Proverbs 24:26 CEV

Chapter #11 – Courage

Have I not commanded you? Be strong and courageous! Do not tremble or be dismayed, for the LORD your God is with you wherever you go. – Joshua 1:9

So we can confidently say, The Lord is my helper; I will not fear; what can man do to me? – Hebrews 13:6

Be strong and courageous. Do not fear or be in dread of them, for it is the Lord your God who goes with you. He will not leave you or forsake you. – Deuteronomy 31:6

I say to you, My friends, do not be afraid of those who kill the body and after that have no more that they can do. – Luke 12:4

Therefore, take up the full armor of God, so that you will be able to resist in the evil day, and having done everything, to stand firm. – Ephesians 6:13

The LORD is for me; I will not fear; What can man do to me? – Psalm 118:6

NOTE: All scriptures are New American Standard translation unless noted.

Scripture References

Chapter #12 – Passion

I can do all this through him who gives me strength. – Philippians 4:13 NIV

Never give up. Eagerly follow the Holy Spirit and serve the Lord. – Romans 12:11 CEV

Let us not lose heart in doing good, for in due time we will reap if we do not grow weary. – Galatians 6:9

Watch over your heart with all diligence, For from it flow the springs of life. – Proverbs 4:23

Do your work willingly, as though you were serving the Lord himself, and not just your earthly master. – Colossians 3:23 CEV

He who loves money will not be satisfied with money, nor he who loves abundance with its income. This too is vanity. – Ecclesiastes 5:10

For the love of money is a root of all sorts of evil, and some by longing for it have wandered away from the faith and pierced themselves with many griefs. – 1 Timothy 6:10

And we know that God causes all things to work together for good to those who love God, to those who are called according to His purpose. – Romans 8:28

Love is more important than anything else. It is what ties everything completely together. – Colossians 3:14 CEV

Epilogue

If you love each other, everyone will know that you are my disciples. – John 13:35 CEV

NOTE: All scriptures are New American Standard translation unless noted.